Andreas von Zadora-Gerlof

The Art of
Zadora

Text by Janet Zapata
Photography by David Behl

The Art of
Zadora
America's Fabergé

The Vendome Press
New York

For more information about Zadora
call 1 (800) 858-2980 (in U.S. only)
or (212) 838-3971, or visit www.zadora.com

Designed by Marc Walter / Bela Vista

Copyright © 1999 The Vendome Press
Photographs copyright © 1999 David Behl, except the
following (numerals refer to page numbers):
Copyright © Gheorghe Adam: 19; copyright © William
Brinker: 27 (both); copyright © Owen Brown: 28 (top);
copyright © Gary Cox: 18, 84, 98 (top), 154, 155 (bottom);
copyright © Rich Frishman: 53; copyright © Helga Photo
Studio: 65; copyright © Eric Landsdowne: 31 (left);
copyright © Marina Merkulov: 28; copyright © John
Parrish: 116, 117 (top); copyright © Larry Stein: 36-42, 43
(bottom), 44, 45, 55, 59, 69, 73 (bottom), 76, 78-83, 92, 93
(both), 101, 103, 118 (both), 127, 129, 143, 144 (bottom), 147
(bottom and left), 148 (bottom), 149, 150 (top), 151 (bottom),
152-53, 156-59, 160 (bottom right), 161-65, 166 (bottom), 169;
copyright © John Wadsworth: 7.

Published in the U.S. in 1999 by
The Vendome Press
1370 Avenue of the Americas
New York, N.Y. 10019

Distributed in the U.S. and Canada by
Rizzoli International Publications through
St. Martin's Press
175 Fifth Avenue
New York, N.Y. 10010

Library of Congress Cataloging-in-Publication Data
Zapata, Janet.
The art of Zadora : America's Fabergé / by Janet Zapata ;
photography by David Behl.
p. cm.
ISBN 0-86565-201-5
1. Zadora-Gerlof, Andreas von–Criticism and
interpretation. 2. Art objects, American. 3. Art objects–
United States–History–20th century. 4. Jewelry–United
States–History–20th century. I. Zadora-Gerlof, Andreas
von. II. Behl, David. III. Title.
NK839.Z34Z36 1999
739.2'092–dc21   99-26516

Printed and bound in Italy

CONTENTS

— 6 —

FOREWORDS

by Christopher Forbes and George E. Harlow

— 9 —

INTRODUCTION

— 21 —

THE MODERN GOLDEN AGE OF GLYPTOGRAPHY

— 55 —

SCULPTED TREASURES

Objets d'Art in Translucent and Opaque Stones

— 107 —

OBJECTS FOR THE HOME AND OFFICE

— 127 —

CLOCKS THAT ALSO TELL TIME

— 147 —

NATURE-INSPIRED JEWELRY

— 176 —

SELECT BIBLIOGRAPHY

— 176 —

NOTES

FOREWORDS

Malcolm S. Forbes began collecting Fabergé in the early 1960s. As a young teenager, I excitedly shared his fascination with the incredible craftsmanship, beauty, and whimsy of these precious objets. Not quite three decades later I was introduced to the work of Andreas von Zadora-Gerlof by the incomparable Eleanor Lambert. I experienced the same pleasure and delight in viewing and handling his exquisite pieces that I had with our first Fabergé acquisitions.

Andreas's sensitivity to the intrinsic qualities of each of the semiprecious stones from which his hallmark pieces are sculpted is without parallel. Since the collapse of Czarist Russia, numerous craftsmen-jewelers have endeavored to imitate Fabergé. Their pastiches are curiously unsatisfying. Andreas's originality is therefore particularly refreshing and intriguing. Not since Peter Carl presided over the House of Fabergé has a maestro enjoyed such harmony with and appreciation of the materials of his chosen métier.

Unlike Fabergé, however, von Zadora-Gerlof is himself the master carver responsible for the whimsical and wonderful sculptures in precious and semiprecious stones that are the hallmarks of his firm's work. It was the near-tragedy of a hunting accident that, in fact, triggered Andreas's incredible talent. As therapy for his son's almost paralyzed right hand, Joachim von Zadora-Gerlof apprenticed Andreas to the noted Haida Indian carver, Gordon Cross. Andreas then further refined his innate talent in Idar-Oberstein, Germany—the gem carving center to which Fabergé "outsourced" some of the hardstone carvings for his firm's production.

Reaching beyond his own lapidary excellence, Andreas's true genius is his ability to inspire and coordinate the talents of metalsmiths, enamelers, jewelers, technicians, and designers (including his gifted and beautiful wife Monica) to create some of the most sumptuous and fanciful objets d'art of the end of the twentieth century. The dazzling results of the meshing of precious materials and the latest mechanical and fiber-optic technology cannot help but delight viewers of all ages. His mechanized masterpieces such as the lapis carousel and the four replicas of the clock tower at the Children's Zoo in Central Park are more reminiscent of the wizardry and scale of Cartier's most ambitious "Mystery Clocks" than of the modest mechanical surprises produced by Fabergé for a few of the Imperial Easter Eggs. The ability to both delight and dazzle is unique to von Zadora-Gerlof in this day and age.

Likewise those wearing Andreas's signature carved hardstone jewelry—from flowers to pheasants, acorns to alligators—bask in the compliments that they invariably receive—an experience which my wife has enjoyed firsthand. Of all the pieces of Andreas's work that we are privileged to have in our own collection, my wife's favorite is a parure. Knowing that Astrid's mother was a Bismarck, Andreas used the acorn and oakleaves of the family crest to fashion a necklace, earrings, and brooch of gold-backed tourmaline leaves and citrine nuts. The result is sublime in its understated elegant naturalism. As is the case with all of Andreas's jewelry, it provides pleasure for both viewer and wearer alike.

Hopefully this splendid book will allow an ever-wider audience to revel in the unique beauty, humor, and brilliance of the work of Andreas von Zadora-Gerlof.

Christopher Forbes

Viewing a carved crystal is always an inspiring treat for me. The skill and understanding required to transform a bulky, complex, and adamantine "stone" into fauna or flora are formidable and rare. Masters of this craft, the glyptic arts, are not many—only a few have recognizable names. From my perspective as a student of crystals and gems, the raw material for stone or gem carving, I appreciate their intrinsic beauty, rarity, and challenge. Some true stones—rocks—have subtle form and texture hiding underneath the surface. These may provide the pattern that will enhance the buffalo or goddess hiding within the stone, but, equally likely, the pattern hides a flaw destined to render the sculpture into fragments. The stone artist must interpret these properties as an engineer and geologist to select the rock whose flaws will work to advantage. With fabulous transparent crystals—aquamarines, rock crystal (water-clear quartz), or tourmaline—the internal patterns are more clearly visible but are more difficult to handle in the hard and fragile substance. Working it is slow, and one false move can fracture the unique and priceless crystal into a worthless set of shards. On top of these problems, the glyptic artist must truly see his or her work locked inside the crystal, awaiting the cutting, grinding, drilling, and polishing that will free the sculpture and reveal the harmony between stone and new form. A feather in the crystal may become a stripe on fly's wing, the color zone a spot on the forehead, while other features will be turned to dust. The artistic process demands crawling into the stone—the stone must reveal itself for the carver to free the form inside.

And the artist must know his subject. As a curator in a natural history museum, I can appreciate the carvings of subjects that are accurate renditions of nature. These are the most emotionally resonant and enlightening. To recognize a tourmaline's color zoning faithfully transformed into a butterfly's wings, or mottled green nephrite into a frog, pink jasper into a pig, brown obsidian into Lutra Lutra, is to understand a great accomplishment by a student of nature in the marriage of mineralogy with biology, inorganic to organic. The consummate artist who can perform these transformations must love both crystal and creature. Consequently, it is a distinct pleasure to introduce you to the marvelous work of Andreas von Zadora-Gerlof, one of those rare and talented artists capable of bringing stone to life.

George E. Harlow
Curator of Minerals and Gems
American Museum of Natural History

INTRODUCTION

Beauty and splendor… no other words in the English language more aptly describe the art of Andreas von Zadora-Gerlof's sculpted gems. Over the past twenty years this gifted artist has created works of art that rival famous gemstone sculptors over the centuries. He is heir to the great masters from classical times, the Renaissance, and, of course, the hardstone sculptors at the House of Fabergé. Von Zadora-Gerlof's ability to turn hard gem material into wondrous objects, often in the guise of animals and plants that seem almost alive, sets him apart from his predecessors. This was brought clearly to the attention of sculpture and jewelry devotees at the Forbes Magazine Galleries exhibition in November 1992 (fig. 1). This show and the accompanying catalogue, entitled *Objects of Desire: The Art in Sculpted Gems of Andreas von Zadora-Gerlof*, demonstrated to the public for the first time the superb work of this talented sculptor. Now, in celebration of his twentieth anniversary of creating works of art in gemstones, it is time to present to a wider audience a more comprehensive view of his oeuvre, as well as a closer look at the artist as a person.

Inspired by a variety of sources of wildlife, from museums, zoos, aquariums, and books, to strolling the grounds around his home on the Queen Charlotte Islands, Andreas von Zadora-Gerlof has captured the essence of nature in his work. Animals of every kind come alive, each figure rendered anatomically correct down to their sinews, tendons, bones, fur, feathers, or scales. Through subtle nuances in facial expressions or body poses, he brings to life the personality of each critter. Mice are meek, pigs are cute, boars are powerful, birds are graceful, and frogs are smug.

Growing up on the mist-shrouded archipelago of the Queen Charlotte Islands, halfway between Vancouver, British Columbia, and Alaska, prepared von Zadora-Gerlof for his life's work. Not only did this idyllic setting allow him access to many species of animals, including birds and fish not seen anywhere else on earth, but it is also the home of the Haida Indians, master boatmen, hunters, and artists. The islands were his playground, and on them he swam, fished, and hunted under the watchful eyes of his parents. He attended the local elementary school with children from the Haida tribe, the noted totem pole carvers.

At the age of twelve, an unfortunate hunting accident forced Von Zadora-Gerlof to turn to wood carving for physiotherapy to help him regain use of his injured right hand. He studied with Gordon Cross, the totem master whom he credits as being his most

2

1. A collection of gemstone sculptures, clocks, and jewelry sculpted from various gem material including citrine, rock crystal, green beryl, aquamarine, labradorite, and tourmaline with 18-karat gold and accented with diamonds, precious gemstones, and enameling.
2. Entrance to "Objects of Desire: The Art in Sculpted Gems of Andreas von Zadora-Gerlof," the first exhibition of Zadora's work, at the Forbes Magazine Galleries in New York City, November 1992.

3

3. "Two Ways to Look at It," 1994. British Columbian jadeite, labradorite, black obsidian, agate, white jadeite, diamonds, garnets, carnelian, 18-karat gold; length: 5'. This sculptural group depicts a topographical map of the Queen Charlotte Islands with representations of the Haida Indian culture portrayed as a raven and the Western perspective as an eagle. Pages 12-13 show reverse view, with sides of birds depicted in the Haida totemic style sculpted in concentric shapes.

important artistic guide. After a relatively short time, Cross realized that his student had the gift of "form-feel," the ability to visualize objects within a raw block of wood or stone.

His close association with Cross reinforced the impact of his earlier exposure to the Haida culture, leaving an indelible mark not only on his artistic makeup but also on his outlook on life. One might say that the Haidas played a key role in the development of his artist's soul. Though his life does not allow him time to travel to the Queen Charlotte Islands, the people and the culture are still very much in his thoughts. In 1994, as a mature artist, von Zadora-Gerlof paid homage to this heritage by sculpting a group he named "Two Ways to Look at It" (figs. 2 and 3). This is not only an awe-inspiring piece to contemplate and admire; it is equally fascinating to hear von Zadora-Gerlof explain what it means.

This work depicts a topographical map of the Queen Charlotte Islands. Von Zadora-Gerlof sculpted the land masses in jadeite and the water in labradorite. Perched on opposite ends of the Island, their wings fully outstretched, are an eagle and a raven, two birds that hold special meaning to the Haida people. The raven is placed at the northeast tip of Graham Island where, according to Haida legend, it discovered the first men hidden in a clamshell (this is also the island on which the artist grew up).

The design of the eagle and the raven dramatically portrays the contrast between the Western and the Haida cultural perspectives that von Zadora-Gerlof experienced throughout his childhood, as he moved between his home environment, grounded in European roots, and the Haida-influenced school and play environment. Looking at the sculpture from one side, the bird figures are rendered in meticulous, naturalistic detail (fig. 2); looking from the opposite side, one sees the body parts sculpted in concentric shapes with soft, rounded curves emanating outwards from a central source–a totemic representation characteristic of the Haida view of the world (fig. 3). The raven, sculpted in black obsidian, perches atop an 18-karat gold moon; the side featuring Haida-style facial features typical of their totemic figure. In Indian folklore the raven pried the clam shell open, freeing man. It is also credited with bringing light, land, and fire to the world. This noble bird gave mankind what it needed to survive. In contrast, the white jade-and-agate eagle clutches a gold salmon in its talons, symbolizing the white man snatching the fruits of the land. The raven gives while the eagle takes away–two different viewpoints from two different worlds–the two worlds of von Zadora-Gerlof.

THE ART OF GLYPTOGRAPHY - THE BEGINNING

Gems fascinate von Zadora-Gerlof as much as they must have prehistoric man several millennia ago. To find a stone that has been formed in the recesses of the earth thousands or even millions of years earlier and sculpt it into an identifiable shape so that its inner beauty comes to light is a challenge accepted by few. Although the art of gemstone carving, known as glyptography, dates back to ancient times, only a few masters have excelled at this demanding craft. It is a physically, mentally, and emotionally draining endeavor in which only the gifted, and strong of body and mind, achieve success. Von Zadora-Gerlof ranks with the best. He brings to this branch of the applied arts a new understanding of and appreciation for this art form. Building on the experiences of his predecessors, his art today exemplifies the heights to which hardstone carving has progressed since its early beginnings. To validate this claim, it is appropriate to trace the history of the fine art of glyptography from its beginnings up to the present day.

Existing records tell us that gem carving began as early as the fourth millennium B.C., making it one of the oldest art forms known to man. Since that time there have been only a few periods in history when this art thrived. By its nature a very technically challenging endeavor, its advancement requires artisans who not only perfect their own skills but also improve the techniques they utilize. Only in rare instances do we find artists with both the proficiency and artistic creativity to elevate the craft to an art form. Of course these artists also require a demand for their work, whether for talismanic or identification purposes as in ancient times, or to accommodate royal patronage in the Renaissance. Throughout the ages, talent and demand must exist simultaneously to bring about the creation of truly remarkable objects. The earliest carvings were small seals, engraved with images for personal use. It was not until the third century B.C. that large vessels were shaped from a single block of gemstone. From these beginnings, the art developed.

People have always expressed their fascination with the unusual nature of gemstones by assigning magical properties to them. It followed naturally that they would want to enhance those magical powers by decorating the gems with various symbols and images, including figures of gods, men, and animals, as well as meaningful inscriptions. Since these stones often functioned as personal seals, the incised design known as "intaglio" held a special meaning for their owners. Each intaglio was a miniature work of art with designs so intricate that they demanded high levels of technical expertise and patience to execute. Many ancient examples have survived and bear witness to the mastery of the lapidary skills. The popularity of objects incised with images continued unabated into the Roman era, when the likenesses of nobles were carved into colored gemstones.

In Mesopotamia, beginning about 3200 B.C. gems were carved into cylinder-shaped seals for purposes of identification. As the skill of the lapidary has grown through the centuries, the standard gem material for these seals has moved from softer stones, such as limestone and serpentine to harder stones such as hematite, quartz crystal, and different forms of chalcedony (the term "hardstone" is used for gem materials that measures 6 and above on the Mohs' hardness scale; these materials have a greater resistance to scratching, which makes them desirable for ornamental carvings). Before the introduction of iron tools around 1,000 B.C., these seals were engraved with copper gravers and simple drills operated by a bow. Some time later the cutting disk was introduced. For hardstones, an abrasive powder such as emery was used to aid the cutting.

The earliest hardstone seals of ancient Egypt date to the end of the Old Kingdom (c. 2680-2260), and are "button seals," a term derived from their general shape. These were soon superseded by seals carved in the shape of the scarabaeus beetle, a symbol of regeneration in the ancient world. Intaglio designs were engraved into the base and around the circumference, with appropriate inscriptions in Egyptian characters appearing beneath the image. These seals served as an amulet and as a signet used to secure valuable prop-

erty against theft, as well as a necessary signatory for anyone owning even the smallest amount of property because without it legal documents were invalid.

By the second quarter of the sixth century B.C., Greek gem engravers had further perfected the art of intaglio carving, using a revolving drill operated by a bow. The finished seals were worn attached to a swivel or suspended as a pendant, a fashion that continued into the classical period. By the fourth century, the scarabeus was replaced with the ringstone, designed for setting into a metal finger ring for use as a talisman or a signet as its predecessors. Intaglios remained popular in Greece into the Roman period.

By the end of the fourth century and into the beginning of the third century, a new kind of carved stone, the cameo, became popular in Greece. Whereas intaglios were engraved with incised designs, cameos were carved in relief, often in a material with layers of different colors that artists incorporated into their designs for greater effect. Unlike seals which fulfilled utilitarian and talismanic purposes, cameos were made purely for aesthetic appreciation and enjoyment, to be worn as personal adornments or displayed in cabinets for the pleasure of their owners.

With Alexander's conquests in the East, more gem material became available for the Greek studios, especially translucent stones that could be cut and set to reflect light. This period also saw the emergence of Alexandria as the center of a new glyptic art form, the carving of hardstone vessels. The earliest trace of such objects is a mention of an onyx vessel "in the context of the Dionysiac ceremonies organized at Alexandria by Ptolemy II Philadelphos (285-246 B.C.)."[1] Within a hundred years, the skill to produce such objects, as well as the desire to own them, had grown to such an extent that the treasury of Mithridates VI, king of the Pontus (120-63 B.C.) contained over 2,000 onyx vessels.[2]

The popularity of carved hardstone vessels quickly spread to Rome, which soon became the center for this trade. By 200 B.C. Rome had become the capital of the greatest empire the world had yet known. Cosmopolitan, architecturally magnificent, and holding the seat of power, it evolved into a city that expressed the dignity and diversity of the state. The grandeur of Rome was reflected in all areas of the arts, from architecture and sculpture to the glyptic arts.

The gem materials used in carving hardstone vessels in Rome were rock crystal, chosen for its lack of color, and agate, particularly sard-onyx, chosen for its multi-layered color qualities. Roman vessels were entirely monolithic–meaning that the entire vessel, including handles and bases, was carved from a single block of stone. The challenge was to carve the entire vessel without error, because one slip of the drill would render the stone useless. Noted characteristics of these early vessels included thin walls, about two to four millimeters thick, scroll handles inspired by plant motifs, and simple, flat bases. Surface decoration, if any, was limited to an occasional concave recess. Natural striations of color from particular stones were the principal decorative accent. By the third century A.D., the surface was further enhanced by gadrooning and fluting.

The glyptic arts flourished in Rome for a long time, but as the empire declined, so did they along with all the arts. By the end of the fifth century only Byzantium actively produced hardstone carving. As in the Classical period, vessels were still carved out of agate, particularly sard-onyx. By the 12th century, semiprecious gemstones had been replaced by non-precious stone material.

Many extant hardstone vessels dating from the Roman period were refashioned into more "modern" pieces during the Byzantine and Medieval periods. The treasury of San Marco in Venice has two sard-onyx chalices with later silver-gilt and cloisonné enamel rim, stem, and foot additions; one bowl dates to the 1st century B.C. and another to the 3rd or 4th century B.C.[(3)] On both, ecclesiastical figures decorate the metalwork added in Constantinople in the mid-10th century.

The idea of utilizing antique gems and vessels of pagan origin onto liturgical vessels was not alien to medieval man, who saw himself as a citizen of the empire founded by Augustus.[(4)] As such, they viewed their history as a continuation of antiquity and did not consider the reuse of ancient pagan relics for religious purposes as an ethical conflict. What mattered to the medieval mind was the permanence of form and aesthetic beauty, as expressed by St. Thomas Aquinas in terms of integrity, symmetry, and clarity. Flawless—or sometimes not so flawless—antique relics were accorded these attributes of beauty, regardless of their prior pagan status.

The reuse of artifacts from previous periods is seen in the Cross of Lothair II in the Cathedral Treasury of Aachen.[(5)] Made around 1,000, possibly for Otto III, the gold cross is set with gemstones, gold filigree work, a Carolingian seal, and a Roman sard-onyx cameo of the Emperor Augustus crowned with a laurel wreath and holding an eagle scepter. The seal and the cameo lent legitimacy to this imperial Ottonian object, establishing a direct line of succession back to the Roman Empire.

The chalice of Abbot Suger, now in the National Gallery of Art in Washington, D.C., is another example of the re-utilization of an ancient artifact.[(6)] A fluted agate cup of Egyptian origin, or, perhaps, Alexandrian dating to the second century B.C., was incorporated into the design of the chalice. The silver-gilt mount from c. 1140 is set with gemstones and pearls.

By the end of the twelfth century hardstone carving had been revived, with rock crystal becoming the preferred material for liturgical vessels. By the next century jasper, agate, and amethyst had been introduced and, by the 14th century, vessels were made not only for church use but also for the rising demand of the secular world, mainly princely patrons.

THE ART OF GLYPTOGRAPHY - THE FIRST GOLDEN AGE

The Italian Renaissance, a period of remarkable artistic accomplishments, witnessed a great resurgence of the glyptic arts. Under the patronage of the Medici in Florence, gem carving was elevated to the status of the ancient jewel carvers. Géza von Habsburg in *Princely Treasures* rightly describes their impact: "… this remarkable family, who emerged from the bourgeois world of apothecaries and merchant bankers to reign as sovereign Grand Dukes, never ceased to collect on an opulent scale, everything from coins, cameos, and jewels to bronzes, mosaics, etched crystal, and colorful hardstone vessels mounted in gold or silver."[(7)]

Lorenzo de Medici, known as Lorenzo the Magnificent, was a true lover of the arts. He often relied upon trusted cultural advisers to help select appropriate pieces and, in the true sense of the Renaissance man, invited talented artisans to Florence to pursue their art. Lorenzo collected old intaglios, cameos, and antique vessels that not only served as sources of inspiration for his engravers but were also modernized with contemporary Renaissance silver-gilt mountings,[8] much in the same way as had been done in the Byzantine and Medieval periods. Upon his death in 1492 the inventory of his collection listed thirty-three hardstone vases with an appraisal value of one-third of his inventoried estate.[9]

The enthusiasm of the Medici for collecting antique objets d'art, combined with a discriminating patronage of gifted contemporary artists, became a dynastic tradition. Successive generations of Medici took Lorenzo's love of art and patronage to new heights. In 1533, when he needed a present for a royal wedding, Cosimo I, Grand Duke of Tuscany, commissioned Valerio Belli of Vicenza, who was known as "the prince of engravers" and who had the gift of "making naturally hard jewels and precious stones soft and tender."[10] Belli created a masterful silver-gilt and rock crystal casket engraved with scenes from the Life of Christ[11] that Cosimo presented to King Francis I for the wedding of his second son, the future Henry II, to Caterina de Medici, who eventually become Queen and, later, Regent of France. Cosimo also invited the celebrated Milanese gem carver and medallist, Giovanni de' Rossi, to Florence. There he executed a cameo of white onyx depicting Cosimo I and his family under a winged figure of Fame blowing a trumpet. It is credited as one of the masterpieces of Renaissance gem carving.[12]

When Francesco I succeeded his father, Cosimo I, as Grand Duke of Tuscany, art and patronage of gifted artists took on a new dimension. He commissioned the designer and architect, Bernardo Buontalenti, to build the Palazzo del Casino di San Marco to house his extensive collection. The Palazzo became a center for artists and craftsmen as well as a place where experiments were undertaken and new techniques invented, such as melting rock crystal and devising a technique for making porcelain. Francesco, an eager participant, was a prince-alchemist, "… the incarnation of a Renaissance prince, dedicated to politics, art and science with equal and balanced zeal."[13] Likewise Buontalenti was not only an architect, but also excelled as a hardstone carver, as evidenced by a magnificent lapis lazuli flask, sculpted with the bodies and wings of harpies on the shoulder, with enameled gold necks and heads.[14]

Thanks to the patronage of the Medici, Italian jewel carving held an unchallenged, long-standing position throughout Europe, from the Renaissance to the Baroque periods, with artists from Florence, Rome, and Milan disseminating the art throughout the continent. And it was the Medici example that inspired other foreign rulers, such as Francis I, Charles V, Philip II, and Rudolf II, to collect not only Italian painting and sculpture but also the glyptic arts.

By the second half of the sixteenth century the Mannerist period was in full swing. Gone was the fascination with the antique, which was replaced by an exuberant, rich style with abundant decorative effects, often bordering on the bizarre. Jewel carving attained a new level of creativity, especially in Milan, where the Saracchi and Miseroni families and Annibale Fontana catered to the major courts of Europe, including Florence, Madrid, Munich, Paris, Prague, and Vienna. Large pieces of rock crystal were brought to Milan, where the gifted carvers created fanciful objects in the shapes of birds and boats. Whether in rock crystal or semiprecious hardstones, vessels were no longer monolithic; most were now assembled from several different parts joined together by elaborate silver-gilt or gold mountings embellished with precious gemstones and pearls. Surfaces became highly decorated with engraved scrolling leaf motifs or other appropriate decorations.[15] These carved vessels were a true feast for the eyes and filled many princely art cabinets, known as *Kunstkammers*, many of which evolved into private museums that served to reinforce the eminence of a ruling house's reign. Ultimately, many of these *Kustkammers* became public institutions.

A noted *Kunstkammer* and treasury that subsequently became the world-renowned museum in Dresden, *Grünes Gewölbe* (the Green Vaults), was established by the House of Wettin, rulers of Saxony. Each member of the house added to what became an extensive collection that rivaled the Medici collection. As the size of the *Kunstkammer* grew, Elector Augustus of Saxony expanded the building project begun by his predecessor, Duke Moritz, and constructed a new west wing on the Dresden palace. Upon its completion in 1554, Elector Augustus converted one floor of the new wing into what was to become the first museum in Europe. Interested in science and the arts, he established the Dresden Cabinet of Curiosities in 1560, laying the groundwork for the Green Vaults. Among the riches housed in his *Kunstkammer* were rock-crystal vases, bowls of jasper and chalcedony, goblets of rock crystal, and vessels in serpentine that had been mined near Dresden.

When Elector Friedich Augustus I, Augustus the Strong, ascended to the throne in 1694, he set out to establish Dresden as a cultural center on a par with Paris, Vienna, or London. He built a new Baroque palace and, in 1721, began to redecorate and enlarge the Green Vaults Treasury. At the center of the new Green Vaults stood the Valuables Room holding the virtuoso creations of Johann Melchior Dinglinger, the court goldsmith who worked in the Mannerist tradition of Benvenuto Cellini and Wenzel Jamnitzer. Dinglinger created elaborate objects, not unlike stage sets, that are true masterpieces in their own right. He worked closely with his brothers, Georg Friedrich and Georg Christoph, as well as other jewelers, enamelers, and sculptors in an atmosphere that was more like an atelier where Dinglinger acted as an impresario staging elaborate extravaganzas.

It was the custom of ruling courts to consolidate claims to their house through the show of impressive works of art, especially the kind whose very making seemed to stretch beyond the limitations of mortal man, appearing almost as if only a god could create such splendor. Such is the case with Dinglinger's most elaborate work, *The Court of the Grand Moghul*. Measuring 56 by 45 inches, it features 132 gold figures of men bringing birthday gifts to the Grand Moghul, as well as an assortment of 32 vases, cups, and other objects all set in a framework of stairs, balustrades, and arches. It is a masterpiece of chinoiserie, the fulfillment of a European vision of the riches and curiosities of the East, combining

Japanese, Chinese, Indian, and Egyptian motifs into one glorious work of art. Completed in 1708, it took Augustus the Strong five years to pay for this extravaganza!(16)

Other works by Dinglinger executed for the Dresden Court, although possibly less ambitious than *The Court of the Grand Moghul*, are no less lavish. *The Bath of Diana* is made up of an ornamental cup of chalcedony with a statuette of Diana, executed by the sculptor Balthasar Permoser, supported by the curving horns of a stag's head with dogs and dolphins, bulrushes and other plants.(17) *The Obeliscus of Augustalis* and *The Altar of Apis* incorporate cameos and intaglios from the Wettin's collection.(18) Such riches as seen at the courts of the Medici and Wettins were not to be seen again until the end of the nineteenth century.

THE ART OF GLYPTOGRAPHY - THE NEXT GOLDEN AGE

The advancement of the glyptic arts had been brought about by a combination of enlightened monarchs or other members of the aristocracy with aesthetic taste and artists with exceptional talent to create innovative works. Such a combination happened again at the end of the nineteenth century when the Romanovs ruled Russia and the gifted designer Peter Carl Fabergé, satisfied their growing desire for beautiful objects.

Fabergé was born in 1846, the son of a prosperous jeweler. Before taking over his father's firm, he studied in London, Paris, Vienna, and Dresden, where he saw first hand the splendors in the Green Vaults. This inspired him to convert the firm's production from diamond jewelry to fantasy objects. Fabergé was the head of a large organization of many workshops. As head of the firm, he confined his attention to designing and overseeing the creation of objects from conception to completion. He personally inspired, directed, and examined the work of his craftsmen through stages of their work. At the height of its fame, the house of Fabergé employed nearly five hundred work masters, including designers, gold- and silversmiths, jewelers, enamelers, and lapidaries.

With Fabergé's gift for creating the beautiful, it's natural that he would turn his attention to objects carved out of hardstones, especially since he had ready access to gem material from the local Russian mines. His preferred stones were agate, aventurine, bowenite, jasper, lapis lazuli, nephrite, obsidian, rhodonite, rock crystal, and purpurine, the latter a transparent purple stone, rarely used in jewelry or gem carving.

Fabergé's fascination with hardstone carving dates to the beginning of his association with his father's firm, in 1870, when he offered a line of gold jewelry in the archaeological style, mounted with hardstone objects. By the next decade, he was commissioning carved stones from Elias Wolff and the Stern workshop at Idar-Oberstein, a town in Germany known for its stone cutting.(19) Fabergé also established a working relationship with Karl Woerffel in St. Petersburg, whose firm became part of the Fabergé enterprise in 1900. There the gem-carvers Kremlev, Derbyshev, and Svetchnikov executed the animals, flowers, and figures for which Fabergé became famous. Fabergé's son, Agathon, was the firm's gem expert and selected the materials for these objects.(20) The work was overseen by Henrik Wigstrom, whose mark is sometimes found on the gold work of Fabergé objects.

Hardstones proved to be the material that enabled Fabergé to elevate functional objects into works of art, often accented with precious and semi-precious gemstones and enamel. Handles for fans, canes, and parasols were fashioned into fascinating shapes while objects such as small boxes, electric bell-pushes, frames, clocks, ashtrays, scent bottles, paper knives, and bonbonnieres became treasures to use as well as to just admire and enjoy. On some of these objects the hardstone was cut to almost as thin as paper and given a high polish to bring out the beauty of the stone.

Along with using carved hardstones for practical objects, Fabergé also created purely decorative objects such as small animals, flowers, genre figures, and, of course, the Easter eggs for which he gained international fame. For animals, he chose stones with coloration patterns that simulated the creatures' natural coats. They varied in size from diminutive pendants to life-size figures. These small bibelots were collected by prominent personages including King Edward VII of England, who, in 1907, ordered models of his horse, Persimmon, several of his dogs, as well as his whole farmyard, which he presented to Queen Alexandra on her birthday the following year.

Winters in Russia were cold and nights were long. To relieve the tedium of the relentless winters, the royal family found delight in small carved objects, especially the small vases of flowers that reminded them of spring. Fabergé flowers replicated actual specimens and were captured at the moment of their blossoming in a variety of gemstones, with nephrite for leaves and rock crystal to simulate water. His genre figures were assembled from various pieces of semi-precious stones. Standing from four to ten inches in height, they depict people from everyday life in St. Petersburg, figures modeled from characters from history and literature, and portrait sculptures.

Perhaps the objects for which the house of Fabergé is best known are the Easter eggs, which were first commissioned by Czar Alexander II, who appointed the house goldsmith and jeweler to the imperial court. This bestowal of favor brought with it an annual commission of Easter eggs. Fabergé produced fifty-six eggs for the czar and his son, Czar Nicholas II, as well as several others for other important personages. These eggs were intricately designed and each contained a surprise inside. They were truly objects of fantasy, made out of precious metals, enamels, and gemstones, with the eggshells often carved from rock crystal and other hardstones. *The Revolving Miniature Egg* in the collection of the Virginia Museum of Fine Arts is fashioned out of two perfect pieces of rock crystal held together by a band of diamonds set into a green enamel mount. The rock crystal serves as a viewing glass through which to see the surprise, twelve intricately painted watercolor miniatures on ivory depicting parks and palaces in Germany, Great Britain and Russia.[21]

With the Russian Revolution and the murder of the Romanovs in 1917, however, the elegance of the imperial court disappeared, as did the firm that had made such beautiful objects. It would be over eighty years before an artistic genius rivaling Fabergé would again make objects fit for royalty.

CHAPTER 1

THE MODERN GOLDEN AGE
OF GLYPTOGRAPHY

Andreas von Zadora-Gerlof descends from Swedish-Baltic ancestry. The von Zadora-Gerlofs lived in the area just south of the Baltic Sea for many centuries. It was not until after World War II, when the Russians and Germans invaded their land, that the family was compelled to move. Von Zadora-Gerlof's parents, Christine and Joachim, emigrated to Canada, settling in Vancouver, British Columbia, where they first had a daughter, Charlotte, and then a son, Andreas, who was born on September 7, 1957.

When his family left their ancestral home they brought with them some of their precious objects from Europe including jewelry, gilt-framed family portraits, and objects by Fabergé including four silver cigarette cases, a rock crystal vase with lilies of the valley, and, as the artist remembers, "… a vicious-looking silver Fabergé toad …" with ruby eyes, resting on a malachite base.[23] The toad belonged to his uncle Peter, who also lived in Vancouver and who would later encourage his nephew to pursue his dream of sculpting.

As the city of Vancouver began to encroach upon their property, in 1963 the family relocated to their four-hundred-hundred acre farm on the Queen Charlotte Islands, known as "The Galapagos of Canada," and built a hunting lodge near the Tlell River, a world-famous salmon stream. This Arcadian land with a plethora of animals proved to be fertile material for Von Zadora-Gerlof when, some years later, he embarked on hardstone carving of animals and other creatures.

Hunting and fishing became his passions and ultimately served as the catalyst for his life's work. Two accidents changed his life forever. One day, while gutting a deer with a knife, the blade slipped, slicing the tendons on the fingers of his right hand. Several years later, while stalking a deer, his hunting companion and friend, Robert Cross, the son of the Haida totem master, accidentally knocked loose a log, which landed on Von Zadora-Gerlof's' right arm and crushed the muscle tissue and tendons. When the cast was removed, his hand resembled a crow's claw. Although he underwent traditional physiotherapy in Vancouver, regeneration did not begin until he started working with

4. Frog Prince, 1995. Bronze, height: 46". The frog riding atop a snail is a metaphor for time passing slowly.

the late Pat McGuire, a noted sculptor who was a friend of Zadora's uncle and who agreed to teach Von Zadora-Gerlof the rudimentary skills of silver engraving. (McGuire has since been awarded the Order of Canada in recognition of his great contribution to native Canadian arts and culture.) When Zadora returned to the Queen Charlotte Islands, the master totem carver, Gordon Cross, recommended additional therapy by practicing the art of sculpting and carving Haida totemic figures. It was here that he learned how to work a cylinder of wood with positive and negative spaces. After studying with McGuire and working with Cross for two years, he felt he had mastered the techniques of engraving on silver, copper, and gold, as well as sculpting wood and, to a limited degree, soapstone and argillite, a relatively soft stone. Von Zadora-Gerlof loved these processes and had found his life's work.

5. Andreas and Monica von Zadora-Gerlof in their New York City apartment.

At the age of sixteen von Zadora-Gerlof left the Queen Charlotte Islands and enrolled in Paige Military School in Los Angeles, an institution his parents hoped would be the groundwork for his life in the military service. In the past, men in the von Zadora-Gerlof family went into military service, and Andreas's father expected his son to continue this tradition. However, after graduation, he returned to the Queen Charlotte Islands for six months, and, with the encouragement of his uncle and James Houston, a friend of his father and a master designer at Steuben Glass, he decided to pursue a career in the glyptic arts. He enrolled in the Gem City College School of Horology and Jewelry in Quincy, Illinois, learning goldsmithing and engraving. At the end of the year he went to Idar-Oberstein, Germany, a center of gemstone carving, to study at the Gemological Institute. While there he saw superb gem engravings of family crests, flowers, and leaves that left an indelible impression on his maturing mind. He remained in Idar-Oberstein after graduation, taking up an apprenticeship in a factory to learn gem cutting and sculpting, as well as working with his teacher, Franz Schichta, who taught him crest engraving.

Von Zadora-Gerlof bought his first lathe at Idar-Oberstein and shipped it home to the Queen Charlotte Islands when he left. Upon arriving home he set up a studio in his family's hunting lodge. His first carved pieces were tiny animals, the first completed piece a rock crystal bird. After a year and a half practicing his art, he began to carve hardstone sprays of flowers, flower and strawberry pins, and crests. He marketed his jewelry in shops in Victoria, British Columbia, and in the gift shop of the Royal British Columbian Museum. To his delight the pieces sold readily. His first private clients were the stage and screen stars, Dudley Moore, whom he met by chance, and Richard Burton. At the outset, von Zadora-Gerlof sculpted small pieces. Gradually, as his self-confidence and skills increased, he worked with larger gemstones. In his own words, "It is so rewarding when you have finished a piece, to know that you have fully used the stone's potential."

Success spurred him to relocate to Los Gatos, in the San Francisco area, where he opened a studio under the name Zadora. One day while walking in the area he noticed a carved moonstone brooch in the window of a jewelry store. He went in, introduced himself to the goldsmith, George Stewart, and ended up selling him a large selection of his jewelry. At about this time he also began working for Arthur Gleim, a respected jeweler and President of the American Gem Society in Palo Alto. A special bench was set up in the window of his store, Gleim the Jeweler, so that passers-by could see Von Zadora-Gerlof at work, carving hardstone sculptures and portrait cameos for clients.

Shortly afterwards he began a collaboration with Stanley Kazanjian at Kazanjian Brothers in Beverly Hills. Together, the two designed special pieces for selected clients. The firm was so pleased with his work that they held special exhibitions to display his latest creations. Mr. Kazanjian, whose family had been in the jewelry business since 1918,

6. The sculptor, Gheorghe Adam, cleaning a rubber mold.

acquired several Zadora sculptures for his own collection. Referring to the artist, Kazanjian remarked, "He can do anything with a block of stone that, for others, would require several stones and the addition of ornamentation."

At about this time, the Los Angeles Zoo sponsored an exhibition of von Zadora-Gerlof's work, featuring endangered animals including specimens of the elephant, wild boar, leopard, and rhinoceros. It was the first time the zoo had held an exhibition of work by a single artist.

Throughout the early stages of his artistic career Von Zadora-Gerlof was blessed with timely advice offered by influential friends and associates who recognized his talent and suggested when and where to make his next moves. He was also blessed with the wisdom to appreciate and follow such advice. In 1985 Robert Crowningshield, head of the Gemological Institute of America, suggested that he work with Ward Landrigan at Verdura. This relationship lasted about a year, during which von Zadora-Gerlof sculpted elements of Verdura jewelry including the head of a unicorn, the torso of a blackamoor, and the bodies of a rhinoceros and an elephant.

His reputation and his success were steadily gaining momentum, from creating small sculptures to co-designing with other jewelers to fabricating one-of-a-kind works of art. His career began to escalate and his name became more widely known. Russell Forgan, a trusted friend and mentor, visited his studio in Los Gatos and encouraged him to relocate to New York City. With the help of Julie Kammerer, Forgan organized his first show at 785 Park Avenue where, again to von Zadora-Gerlof's' amazement, virtually all of his pieces sold. The Southampton show that followed was almost as successful, and was then followed by an exhibition in London.

In 1986 Lincoln Foster of Tiffany & Co. suggested that von Zadora-Gerlof exhibit his work in Paris. While en route, von Zadora-Gerlof stopped in New York, where he met Mil-

lie de Surian, who immediately understood the importance of his work and purchased four pieces. In Paris, he had a one-artist show and sold every piece in addition to taking orders for future commissions. This show generated so much excitement that a special article appeared about him in a Parisian newspaper. Alain Boucheron, from the prestigious Parisian jeweler, Boucheron, came to meet him and, shortly afterwards, a limited business agreement was negotiated whereby Von Zadora-Gerlof would create sculptures to be set into Boucheron's gold mounts and sold under the firm's name. This business relationship lasted about a year.

The Paris show generated sales and also introduced von Zadora-Gerlof to new clients, many of whom have remained steadfast in their enthusiasm for his work. It was also the place where he met a very special person in his life.

The morning after the opening of the show, as Von Zadora-Gerlof was strolling through the streets of Paris, still amazed at his recent success, he walked by the Trocadero, where he saw a beautiful young woman having coffee. He asked the woman if he could join her and exuberantly told her about his recent show. She was a fashion design student from Brazil who had arrived in Paris just two days earlier to study at the Chambre Syndicale de la Couture. It was love at first sight and von Zadora-Gerlof and Monica Shin married three years later (fig. 5). She has become his trusted business associate as well as his valuable design partner. Her first preliminary drawing for "Angelworld" established a working relationship that has consolidated into a powerful team effort with Monica supplying working sketches and practical advice to her artistic husband as his designs evolve from initial conception to implementation.

As a sculptor, von Zadora-Gerlof is always searching for new forms of artistic expression. This quest has taken him beyond the confines of the glyptic arts. About five years ago he met the sculptor Gheorghe Adam (fig. 6) through a mutual friend, leading to a collaborative arrangement whereby Adam provided wax models for jewelry designs. From this beginning, their working relationship has evolved into a partnership for making large-scale bronze sculptures that Adam executes working from Monica's detailed sketches of von Zadora-Gerlof's' designs. They use the *cire perdue* (lost wax) method of casting,[24] which yields figures of exceptional fidelity, as seen in both the Frog Prince astride the snail (fig. 4) and the frog fountain (fig. 7). This form of sculpture enables Von Zadora-Gerlof to create larger pieces (in relation to sizes obtainable from gemstone carving) that can be displayed outdoors in any weather with no loss to the detailing on the figures.

All of von Zadora-Gerlof's creations are conceived three-dimensionally, whether a small piece of jewelry, a large hardstone animal, or a bronze sculpture. The proportions of his figures and objects are balanced with lines flowing naturally. Legs, ears, noses, and other features are never exaggerated, but are accurately rendered and balanced aesthetically from every angle.

His fidelity to nature can be attributed to his years growing up on the Queen Charlotte Islands, which were teeming with animals. Living in this idyllic land gave him an appreciation of and respect for wildlife, resulting in a life-long love of nature. From his

7. Frog Prince fountain, 1994. Bronze, height: 20". The fountain depicts three small frogs and one large frog on a lily pad. When operational, the water spouts at different angles creating interesting trajectory patterns.

8. Frog musicians, 1998. Bronze, approximate height of each frog: 45". The group of frog musicians was inspired by the "music" the artist heard coming from the pond near his home in Victoria, where the frogs "sing" from sundown to midnight. The frog musicians are now on permanent display at the Bronx Zoo.

relationship with the Haida, he learned how to hunt and fish, not for sport but for food. His kills were always properly skinned and gutted, a task that taught him animal anatomy in a practical way that would benefit him when he turned to sculpting. This does not mean that he is a strict representationalist in his approach to art. His animal figures can be quite adventuresome and whimsical while retaining the life-like quality that makes them so appealing.

Sometimes von Zadora-Gerlof borrows elements from different varieties of the same animal or amphibian to give a humorous quality to the figures. Such is the case with the bronze musical frog group (fig. 8). The bodies, with their protruding bellies, are based on the bullfrog or jungle frog, while the hands, feet, and heads are taken from the smaller tree frog. But, as with all of his creations, the proportions have been adjusted to the overall size. Each frog sits on a toadstool, playing his instrument while the conductor raises his left arm, signaling for the music to begin. He sits in a relaxed position with his legs crossed while the musicians perch on their toadstools and play a violin, French horn, harp, cymbals, and a modified balalaika.

Unlike his predecessors, who designed and orchestrated the creation of beautiful objects in a workshop but did not actually make any pieces, von Zadora-Gerlof carves and is otherwise actively involved in every piece himself. The only exceptions to this control are his bronze sculptures.

For especially complex projects von Zadora-Gerlof collaborates closely with his wife, Monica, who makes detailed sketches of his designs, and with a team of goldsmiths, enamelists, lapidaries, and clock makers. Like his predecessors from antiquity, the Renaissance and Baroque periods, and the carvers at Fabergé, he has the requisite talent for his art as well as the patronage to support his efforts. Our late twentieth century rivals other historical periods having astute collectors with the aesthetic appreciation to understand not only traditional painting and sculpture but also the glyptic arts.

Von Zadora-Gerlof has a zest for life, for people, and for art. Fittingly, the Haida tribe from the Queen Charlotte Islands designated him with a name that means "The Involved One." He takes nothing lightly. He enjoys working with people, whether they are his clients or his workmasters. He devotes his full attention to every person or project. He also devotes considerable energy to support larger social issues. After attending a lecture organized by the United Nations about pollution and overpopulation, he felt more interest than ever in the environmental concerns facing our existence and became involved in the Wildlife Conservation Society, which runs the Bronx Zoo. In 1998, he founded the Zadora Wildlife Fund with the purpose of aiding in the preservation of rain forests and other environmentally sensitive areas. For this cause, one of his patrons donated the group of bronze musical frogs (fig. 8) to the Wildlife Conservation Society for permanent display at the zoo. The proceeds from this commission were donated to the Zadora Wildlife Fund.

COMPLEX PROJECTS - THE ZADORA "GUILD"

The art of von Zadora-Gerlof has evolved considerably from sculpting individual or multiple static animal figures to also creating complex, dynamic structures comprising a variety of materials and components working together in perfect harmony. To realize these creations while maintaining his standard of excellence, the artist has assembled a superb team of master craftsmen who, though dispersed geographically throughout the country, work in close collaboration under his direction, taking full advantage of all modern means of communication and transportation, while also making use of all available techniques and devices to build his "impossible" designs. The height to which this team has enabled him to climb is perhaps best illustrated by the elaborate "Four Seasons" clock (figs. 9-11, 16-18, 20-25).

Like Fabergé, Andreas von Zadora-Gerlof makes objects that seem almost impossible to create. And, like his predecessor, he has created an object incorporating eggs with surprises inside. However, since this is the age of technology, his eggs are part of an elaborate clock that not only tells time but also plays a tune while the apparatus rotates and the eggs open and close, revealing four different animated surprises (figs. 17, 21, 22, 25). The theme of this clock, the four seasons of the year, is reminiscent of a subject from the impressionist and art nouveau periods, that of the passage of time. Building on this idea, von Zadora-Gerlof redirected its focus to a late twentieth century environmental theme in which frogs, the first creatures to be affected by changes in the environment, are depicted as marking time on the dial (reminding us that time may be running out) as they support the heavy nephrite base (they bear the weight of the world on their small, fragile bodies). The frog, a dominant figure in this artist's work, also represents his other world, the world of the Haida, in which this creature is the intermediary between land and the sea, living both in and out of the water.

As one contemplates this piece, one is first struck by its sheer size and complexity, combined with the fact that it's made mostly from gems and executed with such exquisite fidelity of detail: the mother hen made out of chirasol, a milky rock crystal; the chicks, rabbits, and squirrels carved from citrine; the carrots from carnelian. Then, observing this beautiful composition in motion, one's sense of wonder grows: after all, the spellbinding beauty of gems is normally static and ornamental. But these gems certainly do move–in fact, they look almost alive. And, when all is in place and operating as planned, it looks and feels not like the clever product of a skillful engineer but rather like a miracle coming from the magic wand of an artist.

In reality, making these pieces look magical takes considerable design and preparation. For single objects, the dominant ingredients are innate form feel and sculpting skills. Sometimes a rare, beautiful gem or stone suggests to the artist a form that will take advantage of its unique qualities; other times, the artist has a specific object in mind and must look for the right stone to bring that object to life, so to speak. In contrast, a complex project requires detailed designing and planning before the artist is ready to remove even the first chip from the first stone. Naturally, the more ambitious the project in terms of scale and mechanical complexity, the lengthier and more detailed the preparation.

9

10

9. "Four Seasons" clock, 1997.
Woods, nephrite, 18-karat gold,
rutilated quartz, guilloche with
transparent enamel; height: 65".
On the hour, the mechanism in the
clock opens an egg to reveal its
surprise, then closes it, rotates, and
opens the next egg, while Vivaldi's
"Four Seasons" plays.
10. Preliminary sketch by Monica
von Zadora-Gerlof of elevation of
"Four Seasons" clock, 1995. Pencil
on paper. Slight variations from the
actual clock include a different
basket-weave pattern on the facade
and a modified base.

12

Von Zadora-Gerlof's' ideas may be triggered by something he observes while strolling in the park, a client's request, or a dream. As the idea germinates, he communicates it to Monica who translates it into progressively more detailed sketches (figs. 10, 18, 23, 24). These sketches are essential, not only to help him refine and make more concrete his artistic concepts, but also to begin identifying skills, approaches, and materials that will enable implementation of those concepts. These sketches eventually become the principal means of communicating project concept and details to the team.

After absorbing the aesthetic impression, it is fascinating to look under the surface of the "Four Seasons" project and learn what went into the actual fabrication of this marvel. How did von Zadora-Gerlof secure and orchestrate the collaboration of his work masters, Gennady Osmerkin, Lew Wackler, Bill Brinker, Jim Hendrickson, and David Monroe, each of whom bring their specialized skills and experiences to the enterprise? It took more than a year to fashion the objects and to put the pieces of the intricate puzzle together so that the clock and figures operate at the striking of every hour or on demand, when a clock wind is turned.

In addition to sculpting each of the animals from gemstones, von Zadora-Gerlof operated as the head work master, coordinating all the steps in the process from initial design to completion. Problems and challenges arose during just about every phase, calling for repeated adjustments. The jadeite plinth was one such challenge. Lew Wackler (fig. 12), in the Boulder, Colorado, workshop, began fashioning the housing out of a piece of jadeite from British Columbia. When he had completed about half of it, he realized that he was not satisfied and made another call to the dealer who happened to have an even better piece in his garden. Out of this second piece, he made courses of blocks of jadeite that he ground and polished until they looked like one piece. Before he could actually carve the desired shape, he created one model in wood and another in plastic.

The other parts of the clock were created by other team members. Victor von Reventlow fashioned the marquetry base from rare and exotic woods. The idea of cabinetry brings to mind tall case clocks, but this is an orbital dial clock (sometimes called a cylindrical clock) which means that time is moved on a short cylinder that rotates in reference to a fixed pointer, instead of the traditional fixed dial with rotating pointers. With a clock like this, telling time almost becomes secondary; the primary focus is the beauty of the object.

11. Detail of "Four Seasons" clock with eggs and celestial armillary sphere. 18-karat gold, guilloche with transparent enamel. The egg for spring is open, revealing a mother hen with her chicks, while a frog marks time beneath the main disk.
12. Lew Wackler, head workmaster, standing next to the Holtzapffel lathe, a machine that cuts regular curvilinear designs into metal, wood, and stone.
13. Bill Brinker, head metalsmith and enamelist, next to a machine that creates guilloche patterns, the engine-turned ground on the metal for enameling.

13

14

14. Gennady Osmerkin, master goldsmith, examining the violin held by the hippopotamus on the "Delacorte" clocks.
15. Workmaster George Merkulov.
16. Work in progress for "Four Seasons" clock in workshop of Gennady Osmerkin.

Every commission is different and requires not only manual dexterity in a given area but also intellectual curiosity to solve the myriad problems that arise. According to Bill Brinker (fig. 13), head metalsmith and enamelist for Zadora's Colorado-based object-making team, "Many of the pieces we produce are assemblages of components made of various materials. Often, each component will require days or weeks of work to complete. It is very exciting to do the final fitting and assembly, which permits us to see the full extent …often for the first time… of our marriage of precious materials."

For the making of every object, there is a story of how it was finally put together, often with parts made all over the world and shipped to the workmaster. For the "Four Seasons" clock, the final assemblage (fig. 16) was accomplished at the shop of Lew Wackler in Colorado. His workshop consists of two lapidaries, Tom Finneran and Ken Sedita, a metalsmith, Kay Conger, and Bill Brinker (fig. 13), who executed the engine turning with transparent enameling on the exterior of the eggs. He also executes all the guilloche with transparent enameling and engine turning for the company. David Monroe from New York City assembled the Swiss-made cylindrical clock in Wackler's workshop, fitting the movement into the casing.

The gold work on the clock was done by three goldsmiths: Gennady Osmerkin (fig. 14), an instructor in jewelry design at the Fashion Institute of Technology in New York City, and the head master of his workshop, George Merkulov (fig. 15); and Jim Hendrickson, a gemologist who works in San Jose and is a past president of the American Gem Society in California. Osmerkin designed the visual assemblies, the chapter rings on each egg, and the still lives. He worked to meld the mechanics and the aesthetics and, ultimately, to make this beautiful clock run properly for the next few hundred years. He is credited with creating the five frogs, the flowers (fifty-six in all), insects, carrot tops, and the tree trunk, as well as the mechanisms for the opening and closing of each egg. He also executed the intricate enameling of the objects contained inside the eggs.

For the "Four Seasons" clock, Jim Hendrickson (fig. 19) created the chicken's nest by hammering, annealing, and hammering each piece of gold straw repeatedly until all were in place before finally texturing each strand. He brings to his craft a level of accuracy measurable to a tenth of a caliper–that is, to the perfection of ten-power magnification. Hendrickson executed the texturing and detailing on the

15

clock, including carving the outer chapter ring with 147 *fleur de lys*, a design that took eight days to make.

The finished clock is a masterpiece in design and craftsmanship representing the best of hardstone carving, goldsmithing, enameling and clock making. Nothing made in this century rivals its combination of technical virtuosity and artistic achievement. It is a true work of art, in which each detail has been carefully considered from conception to execution to contribute to the overall effect. When the hour is struck, the main disk begins its rotation, with eggs opening and closing to the tune of Vivaldi's *Four Seasons*. (A clock wind underneath the jadeite structure can be pushed to activate the movement of the eggs [fig. 20].) The shells of each of the four eggs have been finished in guilloche with transparent enamel in color tones symbolic of a particular season (figs. 17, 21, 22, 25). Each egg

opens, revealing an animated surprise that moves as the shell rises–then reverses this movement as the shell closes. Spring is green, the season of rebirth, and, since the egg is the symbol of creation, it is fitting that the surprise inside should be a mother hen with her chicks (figs. 17, 18). As the egg slowly opens, egg shells crack open and chicks emerge; when it closes, the chicks re-enter their eggs. Summer is red, the season of heat;

this egg opens to reveal flowers growing, opening their petals while a ladybug and a bee buzz around the enameled flowers (fig. 21). Fall is orange, the color of autumn leaves and the harvest; the surprise is two rabbits with carrots with enameled tops that grow right before their eyes (figs. 22, 23). Winter is pale blue, the color of ice; the

19

surprise is hidden underneath the snow-covered tree stump-squirrels hibernating in their lair, surrounded by their nuts (figs. 24, 25). It is a time of regeneration.

Another noteworthy clock executed by von Zadora-Gerlof and his workmasters is the "Delacorte" clock (figs. 26-29), commissioned by a client, with replicas in other gemstone materials for her three children. The actual structure and animals are based on the "Delacorte" clock, located at Fifth Avenue and 64th Street in New York's Central Park. Before beginning this monumental task, von Zadora-Gerlof visited the Hall of Records in City Hall to examine the sketches and photographs of the original clock. He then had a plaster maquette made of the clock and each ani-

18

17. Egg representing spring. 18-karat gold, guilloche with transparent green enameling, chirasol, citrine, white opaque enamel. A mother hen attends her chicks as they hatch from their eggs.
18. Preliminary sketch by Monica von Zadora-Gerlof for spring egg. Pencil on paper.
19. Jim Hendrickson, master goldsmith, putting the final touches on a piece of jewelry.
20. Clock wind for "Four Seasons" clock. Wyoming jadeite, 18-karat gold, guilloche with opalescent white enamel, cabochon amethyst, steel; length: 4".

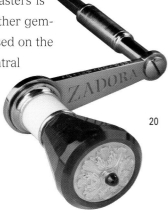

20

21. Egg representing summer. 18-karat gold, guilloche with transparent red enamel, guilloche with various colored enamel, white and yellow diamonds. The flowers grow out of the ground while a ladybug and bee buzz around.

22. Egg representing fall. 18-karat gold, guilloche with transparent orange enamel, citrine, carnelian, cabochon rubies, transparent green enamel. Rabbits watch as carrots grow out of the ground.

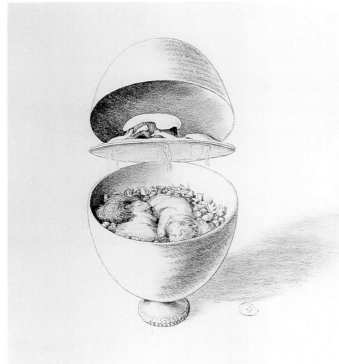

23   24

23. Preliminary sketch by Monica von Zadora-Gerlof for fall egg with rabbits and carrots. Pencil on paper.
24. Preliminary sketch by Monica von Zadora-Gerlof for winter egg with tree trunk and hibernating squirrels. Pencil on paper.
25. Egg representing winter. 18-karat gold, guilloche with transparent pale-blue enamel, opaque enamel, citrine, tourmaline. Squirrels with nuts they have collected are hibernating in their lair underneath the root system of a snow-covered stump.

mal so that his creation would be as close to the original as possible with a few modifications. The four clocks are executed in the following materials: lapis lazuli with citrine animals (fig. 26); apple green Wyoming jadeite with agate animals (fig. 27); banded chalcedony from South Africa with rose quartz animals (fig. 28); and rhodochrosite with multi-gemstone animals (fig. 29).

Each of the clocks stands about five feet tall, with six-inch animal musicians sculpted in translucent gemstones mounted on top. Each musician plays a different gold-and-enamel instrument. The goat plays a modified double English horn; the hippopotamus, a violin; the bear, a tambourine; the mother kangaroo, a French horn while her baby in her pouch plays a cornet; the penguin, a drum; and the elephant plays an accordion. At every hour, two monkeys strike a bell on top of the hardstone clock tower, beginning the rotation of the disk where, as it turns, each animal dances around in a circle to the tune of Beethoven's "Ode to Joy." Vases with bouquets of carved gemstone flowers are set at the four corners.

The actual form of the clock base is loosely based on the walls that surround the clock in Central Park. Two niches on the original have been transposed onto the clock on all four sides, helping to break up the regularity of the brick-like wood marquetry. Each niche is framed by a Roman arch with a keystone. The niches on the front and rear contain rock crystal vases filled with either a bouquet of lilies of the valley on the rhodochrosite clock or mixed flowers in various stones to complement the colors of the animals on the other clocks. A dancing bear and a goat in the other two niches replicate similar animals in niches on the original clock.

If there is one word to describe the allure of these objects, it is fantasy. The end of the twentieth century has witnessed a resurgence of fantasy in the arts, especially film. Both in movies and in the works of von Zadora-Gerlof, this appeals to our aesthetic vision of wonderment. Such is the case with a very special commission by a gentleman who, as a small boy growing up in New York City, did not have the few pennies required for a ride on the carousel. He vowed that someday he would own one himself. As he grew older and more prosperous, he contributed to preserving antique carousels *in toto*, thereby preventing them from being dismantled and sold in separate pieces. Along with his gift came the proviso that the carousels had to be available free of charge to all children one day every year.

The dream to own his own carousel was finally realized in a miniature created by von Zadora-Gerlof (figs. 30, 31, 33). Like real-life carousels, this one is fully mechanized with gemstone animals that prance up and down as it turns. The animals are spotlighted by fiber optics hidden in the poles, and the digital audio music box plays one of twenty different tunes as the carousel turns. Its charms resemble those of real carousels, as its creator points out, "It's remarkable that everyone immediately picks out a favorite animal,

26. "Delacorte" clock, 1996. Lapis lazuli, citrines, tourmalines, diamonds, 18-karat gold, enamel; height: 60". The design of these clocks is based on the Delacorte clock in Central Park, at Fifth Avenue and 64th Street. Beethoven's "Ode to Joy" plays at the striking of every hour.

27. "Delacorte" clock, 1996. Apple-green Wyoming jadeite, agate, citrines, tourmalines, diamonds, 18-karat gold, enamel; height: 60".

26

just as if you were right there at the amusement park waiting for the creature you want-ed to ride." The artist's favorite is a translucent aquamarine morganite seahorse with a blue head, pink belly, and tail. Other animals include a translucent pink quartz pig, a cit-rine ostrich captured in a ballet position with foot raised, a dark-red rubelite sea mon-ster and a frog of green beryl with a saddle on its back (fig. 33). Like the original carousel, reflecting mirrors surround the center, except that here von Zadora-Gerlof fashioned mirrors of white gold.

Von Zadora-Gerlof does not always wait for a commission to begin a special piece. Sometimes he comes up with an idea and, hopefully, a client will understand and love it as much as he does. Such is the case with "Angelworld" (figs. 34, 35), a special piece that he envisioned as a globe supported by angels. He had been contemplating the piece for quite a while but, because of other commitments, had not been able to fully realize it. He described the concept to his then fiancée, Monica, who made a preliminary sketch to cheer him up while he was in the hospital. The drawing so effectively captured the essence of his vision that he immediately looked forward to starting work on the project. Since then, Monica has been sketching his creative ideas on paper so successfully that

Following pages
28. "Delacorte" clock, 1996. Banded chalcedony, rose quartz, opal, diamonds, 18-karat gold, enamel; height: 60".
29. "Delacorte" clock, 1996. Rhodochrosite, aquamarine, citrine, chirasol, rutilated quartz, milky rose quartz, smoky quartz, diamonds, 18-karat gold, enamel; height: 60".

27

goldsmith Jim Hendrickson commented, "She is such a tremendous draftsperson that it seems easy to turn her two-dimensional drawings into three-dimensional objects."

When a client saw the sketch, she was struck by how "his vision of angels and the world created a powerful symbolism for her ... peace in the home could extend to peace on the planet."[25] The etched globe and cloud at the base are sculpted from rock crystal while the five angels are carved from rose quartz with 18-karat gold wings. The client requested that additional figures of birds, frogs and flowers in colored gemstones be added to the cloud for color contrast (fig. 35).

Even though relatively small in number, Von Zadora-Gerlof's' major commissioned projects have been a powerful driving force behind his overall development as a artist. Unafraid of tackling designs requiring considerable technological sophistication, he has shown a remarkable talent for reaching new aesthetic peaks as he conquers the technical challenges. His current "Aquarium" clock project is a good example of how this artist works.

At the time of this writing, the "Aquarium" clock has just been commissioned. With the aid of Monica's sketch (fig. 39), von Zadora-Gerlof has been able to overcome technical obstacles and achieve a truly phantasmagorical design that goes beyond his other commissions in its illusionism, reminiscent of, yet surpassing, the art deco clocks by the French jeweler Cartier, on which the hands seem to move without any visible mechanical means.

On von Zadora-Gerlof's other special-commission clocks, as well as on the carousel, parts rotate, turn, or move up and down, each piece connected to gears or other mechanical devices. The movable parts on the "Aquarium" clock (fig. 38) are not visibly attached to any supporting mechanism, creating the illusion that the fish are swimming in water. This fantasy will be realized by attaching carved hardstone fish to rock crystal tubes that,

32

31. Detail of carousel.
32. Preliminary sketch by Monica von Zadora-Gerlof of "Zodiac" clock, 1997. Pencil on paper. The citrine figures will dance around a citrine turtle, aquamarine globe, and platinum orbital dial clock.
33. Carousel frog, 1991. Green beryl, 18-karat gold, diamonds, rubies, sapphires; height: 2 3/4".

Previous pages
30. Carousel, 1991. Carousel of lapis lazuli, malachite, rhodochrosite, camarra stone, nephrite, rock crystal; animals of watermelon tourmaline, green beryl, aquamarine-morganite, citrine, red tourmaline, orthoglas, rutilated quartz, smoky quartz, rock crystal; platinum, 18-karat gold, diamonds, rubies, sapphires; height: 17 1/2".

33

34. "Angelworld," 1987.
Rock crystal, rose quartz,
pink, blue, and green
tourmaline, yellow
sapphire, 18-karat gold,
colored diamonds;
height: 10".
35. Detail of "Angelworld,"
1987.

34

at the striking of every hour, turn either clockwise or counterclockwise. Special oil floating in the tank will disguise two large rock crystal tubes near the perimeter and three in the center. The rock crystal aquarium will be filled with swimming fish carved from transparent stones of tourmaline, aquamarine, citrine, green beryl, and ametrine while the sand-crawling sea creatures will be executed in opaque stones of agate and jasper. The clock will be set into an octopus resting on the floor of the tank, hours and minutes read through his eyes. The octagonally-shaped tank will rest on a lapis lazuli base, supported by gold dolphins.

CURRENT PROJECTS ON THE DRAWING BOARD

Andreas von Zadora-Gerlof continuously generates new ideas for putting his talents to work. In the middle of almost impossible time pressures to meet current commitments, he somehow manages to add to his creative stream and advance his new ideas along the arduous road to their realization. Current new projects include a zodiac clock, a chess set, and a Christmas tree and crèche, all of which will require the skill of several workmasters.

36

36. Preliminary sketch by Monica von Zadora-Gerlof for Christmas tree and crèche, 1997. Pencil on paper. The Christmas tree will be made in either jadeite or textured 18-karat gold and will be decorated with carved gemstones and enamel ornaments that can be detached and worn as jewelry.

The "Zodiac" clock (fig. 32) is named for the astrological figures sculpted out of citrine or solid gold that, on every hour, will dance about a citrine turtle with an aquamarine globe with gold continents on its back. A platinum orbital dial clock will be set within the globe. The base of the clock will be lapis lazuli. The chess set (fig. 37) will be designed with frogs carved out of jadeite and costumed in 18-karat gold and enamel outfits. The chess board will be made out of black and white jade. The Christmas tree and crèche (fig. 36) will be made out of 18-karat gold with carved gemstone ornaments, mounted with 18-karat gold, and encrusted with diamonds and other precious gemstones. They will be able to be detached and worn as jewelry.

One new area of hardstone carving von Zadora-Gerlof is preparing to pursue is architectural interiors, utilizing gem material to create decorative borders. About fifteen years ago he met two people who were also interested in this pursuit. They both have become friends who not only intend to work on such designs in the future but have also collected his work. When Juan Pablo Molyneux, an architectural and interior designer in New York City, met von Zadora-Gerlof, he was immediately impressed with his work. He observed, "Andreas takes a stone and gives a different meaning to the material … gives it energy." Von Zadora-Gerlof has also been working with Stephen Stefanou, who runs a design firm in Dallas, on plans for architectural uses for hardstones, including veneering mantle pieces, pilasters, and columns in gem material. Stefanou, like many admirers of the artist, cannot have just one example of his work because he "enjoys the passion in the pieces." An additional architectural project in the works will utilize malachite, rock crystal, and lapis lazuli elements and objects throughout the main entertainment areas for a European property (figs. 40, 41).

The remainder of this book is devoted to the presentation of a representative sample of the oeuvre of von Zadora-Gerlof. As is the case with most such expositions, there is no unique or clearly "best" way to categorize a production as vast and varied as this artist has generated in the twenty years since he started as a glyptic sculptor. For example, there are themes and motifs that run across his entire oeuvre. The same is true concerning his utilization of gems. The choice made here is to group his work into four major types of objects: Sculpted Treasures: Objets d'Art in Translucent and Opaque Stones; Functional Objects for the Home and Office; Clocks that Also Tell Time; Nature Inspired Jewelry.

As I discuss von Zadora-Gerlof's work in these four chapters, I will keep in mind the three fundamental ingredients that determine the success of any work of the plastic arts: medium, design, and execution. Combinations of these three interrelated ingredients provide an almost infinite range of possibilities, as a visit to any museum or private collection will reveal. And, of course, there is also a wide range of individual tastes when it comes to assessing the merits of any one piece of art, so that even for works widely recognized as masterpieces, one will hear dissenting opinions on the artist's

37. Preliminary sketch by Monica von Zadora-Gerlof for chess set, 1996. Pencil on paper. The frogs will be carved from jadeite and dressed in 18-karat gold costumes. The set is designed to be fully mechanized.

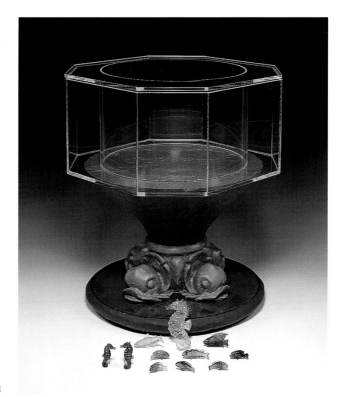

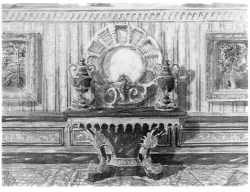

38

40

38. First stage of the maquette for the "Aquarium" clock, 1999. Acrylic, modeling clay, wood, and undersea animals of tourmaline, aquamarine, green beryl, amethyst.
39. Preliminary sketch by Monica von Zadora-Gerlof for "Aquarium" clock, 1998. Pencil on paper.

choice of materials, the wholeness or novelty of the design, or the perfection of the execution (or, even, all of the above).

Ultimately, we are not after producing a score or a rating of different works of art relative to one another. Rather, we use a frame of reference to help us understand the choices made by the artist and thus enhance our appreciation and enjoyment of his work. Since von Zadora-Gerlof utilizes gemstones and other precious materials, there is not much of a question about his chosen medium. At the same time, even cursory examination of any of his pieces reveals that his attention to execution of details borders on perfection. However, we can get much insight and pleasure by examining how his specific choices of gem material and execution of details help him bring the most out of his design concepts. We can also appreciate how capturing live expressions as he sculpts his creatures is one of the key contributions of his designs to the glyptic arts. This book will use these elements shared by all plastic arts to guide you through this enhanced appreciation of his art.

39

40, 41. Architectural plans showing gemstone and hardstone application for a European estate by Kris Novak, 1998. Watercolor on paper.

41

CHAPTER 2

SCULPTED TREASURES

Objets d'Art in Translucent
and Opaque Stones

For several millennia, gemstones have been revered for their magical properties, and prized beyond all other objects. In more recent times, advances in the study of natural history have yielded a thorough understanding of gem material on a scientific level. We know, for example, that most natural gems are mineral substances, pearls and amber being the best-known exceptions. We also know that, with the notable exception of diamonds, which consist solely of carbon, all gems are composed of two or more chemical elements. Beyond these simple facts, the nature and physical properties of gems can get quite complicated and are of no great interest to the average person. However, some understanding is not only fascinating in itself but can be quite useful to better appreciate the variety, beauty and value of gems. This knowledge is vitally important to those who play a role in the transformation of natural gem material into a beautifully carved object or a piece of jewelry.

Most gemstones are essentially crystals that exhibit well-defined atomic structures aligned along imaginary lines, or crystal axes intersecting at the gem's center. These structures determine key physical properties of interest to the glyptic artist, such as hardness, coloration, strength, and preferred direction for clean cleavage (this last property is all-important to the gem cutter). In contrast, opals are amorphous minerals lacking any distinguishable crystal structure (which does not make them any less attractive to the glyptic artist).

Hardness, the degree of resistance against penetration of foreign matter, is a valuable asset for a finished piece but, of course, also a challenge to the artist working the gemstone. Some crystals exhibit different degrees of hardness along different axes, thus increasing this challenge. Diamonds, in addition to the virtues that make them so desirable for jewelry, are also the hardest gems made by nature, by a very large margin. For this quality, they are used to great advantage in gem-carving tools.

The most important qualities in determining the suitability of a gemstone for carving purposes are transparency, luster, color, and "fire." A stone is transparent when light rays

42. King Frog atop toadstool, 1996. Rock crystal, rutilated smoky quartz, diamonds, orange sapphires, 18-karat gold, guilloche with transparent green and white enamel, rock-crystal base; height: 8". The rock-crystal base and sculpted King Frog present a strong contrast to the brightly enameled toadstool.

43. The sculpting process, beginning on the right with a block of stone, roughing out the shape of a goat, completing the form and detailing, and the finished piece after it has been polished. Rock crystal, citrine, rutilated quartz; height of finished piece: 6".

43

pass through it without being refracted. Reduced transparency is referred to as translucency, while a dense, impenetrable stone is denoted as opaque. When light falls on the surface of a gemstone, it partly penetrates and partly reflects against the surface. The reflected rays cause the shine, or luster quality.

Color, perhaps the primary quality of a gemstone, depends on the manner in which the stone absorbs light. The colors we see are those reflected, not absorbed, a property that depends on chemical composition, the nature of impurities present, and often the angle of observation with respect to the crystalline structure. Certain stones, such as malachite and lapis lazuli, maintain a particular characteristic color and are known as idiochromatic stones. Allochromatic stones are colorless in their purest varieties but, with the addition of so-called transition elements, exhibit a wide range of colors. Fire refers to the dispersion or the break up of light as it passes through the stone. In general, the wider and richer in the color the spectrum, the more precious the stone becomes.

With so many possible combinations of physical and chemical properties to work with, nature offers an enormous variety of gem materials. The gem carver selects a stone based on its color, or lack of color, size, and shape, often looking for particular features, such as natural rutilations, distinctive colorations, or absence of any visible imperfections. And, as Andreas von Zadora-Gerlof will tell you, to find that particular gem and cut it into a recognizable shape is almost as difficult as its subsequent carving. Von Zadora-Gerlof often travels around the world or contacts specialists in the field to find just the right stones for a specific piece. As he does so, he also keeps an alert eye for particularly fine specimens he may put aside for future projects. He also relies on a few trusted dealers who regularly visit gem mines and other sources and have access to some of the finest gem material in the world.

To be able to find a gem and carve it into a work of art is a special gift. Von Zadora-Gerlof has been blessed with the ability to visualize an object within a block of stone, a talent known as "form-feel." This proficiency is inborn to all great sculptors. Before taking hammer to marble, the most famous Renaissance sculptor, Michelangelo, envisioned

David, poised and watching the approaching Goliath, within a fourteen-foot marble slab. This piece of marble had stood outside the Cathedral in Florence for forty years, an abandoned project by another sculptor. It would take the genius of Michelangelo to create this artistic masterpiece that captured all the tension and expectation of the act about to be committed. Only a truly gifted sculptor has the ability to not only carve a stone but also to intuitively see the "hidden" shape inside. Very few achieve this level of artistry.

Whereas marble sculptors carve away the stone using chisels and hammers, hardstone sculptors use saws and grinders. Both remove excess material, seeming almost to free the sculpture from within the stone. When von Zadora-Gerlof looks for appropriate gem material, he keeps in mind several factors that will either make the carving easier or more difficult. From his background in gemology, he can identify the crystalline axes of each stone as a guide to where the stone can and cannot be cut. Then he must check for internal cracks or fissures that may weaken a stone, causing it to break apart at an inopportune moment. Or, if there is a visible fissure that is secure (meaning that it will not break), he must determine whether or not this imperfection will be detrimental to the intended aesthetics of the finished piece. He looks for gem material with the fewest fissures but prefers stones that have some slight "ghosts" or "veils," slight imperfections that add visual enhancement and give a stone its individual personality.

44. Andreas von Zadora-Gerlof using a spindle to sculpt details on an aquamarine frog.

After selecting the appropriate gemstone for a project, he begins the arduous task of shaping and carving the stone. There are several steps in carving a three-dimensional object, beginning with a block of stone and ending with the finished object (fig. 43). Before he begins cutting, von Zadora-Gerlof draws the general design on the block of stone, using a felt-tip pen or grease pen. The key step at this stage is to identify where to make the first cut.

After he has determined the entry into the stone, he makes the first cut, which is his first "window" into the interior of the stone. The first two or three such cuts are the most important because, as windows, they allow him to see any flaws and assess any other potential problems inside the stone. He can then conceptualize how to use these imperfections to his advantage as he cuts further into the material. For example, there may be striations he can use for the neck of a small animal or a sea creature such as a turtle. After examining as much of the interior as he can through these windows, he saws the block of stone to remove the excess material as he blocks out the desired shape to be carved. This can be seen in the first carved shape of the goat he has "freed" from the original block of citrine. Using a hand-held grinder, he then continues to remove material until a rough image of the desired object emerges.

In the next step, he uses a stationary grinder to remove more material in a much more controlled manner. He progressively changes the points and wheels to finer ones as he reduces the dimensions of the sculpture to near its final proportions. When he is carving an animal, a fish, or a bird, he must remember to leave a sufficient amount of gem mate-

44

45. Birds in Cherry Tree, 1989.
Aquamarine, blue, green, and red
tourmalines, rutilated smoky
quartz, diamonds, 18-karat gold,
smoky quartz base; height: 8 1/4".
The artist envisioned a caring
family with baby birds in the tree,
protected by their parents.
Following pages
46. Pegasus sculptures, 1997.
Aquamarine, citrine base; height:
15". The superb gem material for
these sculptures came from the
area of Minas Gerais in Brazil.
The original rough stone weighed
180 pounds.

rial around the body from which he can later cut back the hide texture, the scales, the feathers, or any other surface.

To achieve the fine detailing seen on all his sculpture, von Zadora-Gerlof uses a tool driven by a flexible shaft, which is in essence a variation of a dentist's drill (fig. 44). When working with the saw and grinder he holds the piece of stone in his hand, bringing it to the stationary tool, but when operating with the flexible shaft he holds the tool in his hand, slowly moving it around the sculpture. Since this tool operates at a high rotational speed, it can cut away the material very quickly and, in the hands of an expert, very accurately. Using a hand-held tool with the object on the table also greatly reduces the risk of breakage. Throughout the carving process, the artist must drip water or oil onto the stone to reduce the heat caused by friction between the tool and the gem material in order to keep the stone from breaking or cracking. The liquid also rinses away the ground-off material giving him a clean view of the stone surface at all times. Once he's finished sculpting, von Zadora-Gerlof will often let the piece sit for a few days, returning with fresh eyes to see any details that may need retouching or an area that should be reworked.

A key ingredient in this process of abrading away excess gem material is the utilization of diamond dust, cindered or coated onto bits. The interchangeable bits are attached to the saws, grinders, spindles, and flexible shafts and can either be purchased ready-made or the diamond-dust mixture can be prepared in the studio. If processed in the shop, industrial diamonds are ground into powder by use of a mortar and pestle. The pestle with the diamond dust is held against the spinning tool and the diamonds are coated onto the steel in an oil slurry. Diamonds, one of the hardest known substances, can cut almost anything. They provide the perfect grit to cut hardstones and allow the sculptor to achieve intricate detailing.

All the scratches and marks made by the saws, grinders, spindle, and flexible shaft are smoothed out through the use of polishing compounds on leather wheels and brushes of decreasing size charged with grit. The next step is polishing with progressively finer compounds either in the form of a sanding cloth or loose abrasive grain on wood, leather, felt, or cloth buffs. Von Zadora-Gerlof uses a polishing agent such as serium oxide until the object has achieved a high polish and no scratches are visible to the naked eye.

Sculpting in gem materials can be exasperating as it is rewarding, since one slip of the drill can really alter a piece. However, the results can be as spectacular as the pair of aquamarine Pegasus sculptures mounted on a citrine base (fig. 46). Both figures are carved from a single piece of aquamarine, weighing almost 180 pounds. Standing fifteen inches in height, it is perhaps the largest known aquamarine sculpture in existence.

Aquamarine is the name given to bluish beryl, the rock-forming silicate that gets its color from aluminum oxide. It is basically the same stone as emerald, except for the color. The name aquamarine comes from two Latin words: *aqua* meaning water, and *mare* meaning sea, which alludes to the stone's sea water blue-green color. The value of aquamarines depends chiefly on its color: pale, almost colorless stones are readily available while good blue stones are fairly rare. The stone used for the Pegasus group is an extremely rare stone. The rough crystal came from the world-renowned Minas Gerais, Brazil, that produced some of the finest gem material available anywhere.

47. Frog, 1990. Cut from rare crystal of morganite and aquamarine, cabochon rubies, 18-karat gold; height: 2 1/2".
48. Frog, 1989. Fine green beryl, cabochon rubies, 18-karat gold; height: 2 1/2".
49. Coiled snake, 1988. Green beryl, canary diamonds, platinum; height: 1".
50. King Frog atop toadstool, 1991. Aquamarine, cabochon rubies, cabochon sapphires, diamonds, rubelite tourmaline, 18-karat gold, rutilated smoky quartz base; height: 7".

On these sculptures the even color distribution throughout the bodies testifies to the excellent quality of the original stone. Von Zadora-Gerlof has used the variations in the stone's color to advantage. The bodies are translucent while the legs and wings are transparent, resulting in a wonderful play of light. The pose of each Pegasus with its tail on the ground, one leg raised, head up, and wings extended, is evocative of the winged horse of Greek myth that Perseus rode when he rescued Andromeda, and that Bellerophon rode when he slew the chimera.

Aquamarine sculptures can be large or small. Von Zadora-Gerlof also chose this stone to carve the family of birds in Birds in Cherry Tree (fig. 45). In his words, he was "enchanted by the theme of a caring family" and portrayed this theme in this sculptural group. He wanted to make a work with simplicity of design enhanced by color. He achieved this goal by contrasting the pale blue of the birds with the rutilated smoky quartz nest and the dark tourmaline colors of the leaves and berries. The textured gold tree and branches provide support for the carved elements.

For King Frog (fig. 50), von Zadora-Gerlof chose a greener aquamarine, more in keeping with the natural color of the frog. King Frog's throne is a rubelite tourmaline toadstool with a gold stem supported by a rutilated smoky quartz base. Although aquamarine is basically a transparent stone, the stone is sculpted so as to make it more translucent, similar in tone to other such gemstones. As sovereign of his land, King Frog wears a jewel-set gold crown on his head while holding a gold globe in one hand and a jewel-set gold scepter in the other. Von Zadora-Gerlof has also created King Frog in rock crystal sitting atop an enameled toadstool (fig. 42).

For the small sculpture of a frog (fig. 48), the artist chose a fine green beryl that closely simulates the color of the creature. Slithery creatures also work well in beryl, as seen in the sculpture of a coiled snake (fig. 49). To replicate the skin, he carved diagonal lines with cross-hatching across its body. Even at merely one inch in height, this sculpture still projects a monumental feeling, as if the snake were actual size. The ability to make a small figure appear larger requires a level of expertise that very few sculptors achieve.

A rose pink beryl is known as a morganite, named after J. Pierpont Morgan, who presented a large collection of gemstones to the American Museum of Natural History at the turn of the century. Von Zadora-Gerlof created the tree frog sitting on a rock (fig. 47) out of a very rare bi-colored stone that is half morganite and half aquamarine. He has polished the sculpture to heighten its transparency. The poses of the frogs mentioned above, with their legs on one side of the rock as if about to spring up, is reminiscent of similar amphibians by Fabergé's workshop in which a frog sits astride a base with one leg hanging down. Von Zadora-Gerlof created variations on this theme including a jasper frog atop a geode agate base.

48

51. Frog, 1997. Rock crystal, green tourmaline, 18-karat gold; height: 8 1/2", length: 18". The surface of the frog has been minutely detailed, replicating the amphibian's actual skin.

52. Leghorn rooster, 1991. Rock crystal, red tourmaline, opals, canary diamonds, 18-karat gold, rock crystal base; height: 22". A few gold feathers have been added to the rock crystal tail to give color contrast as well as to accentuate the bird's ruffled feathers.

Beryls do not have any specific line of cleavage, so the carver must hope to start on the right path or the piece can split and be lost. For this reason, very few carvers use this material. As an attractive alternative, fine specimens of quartz are more readily available than beryl and significantly more forgiving during the carving process.

Nature offers many varieties of gems in the quartz family, all sharing similar physical properties and chemical composition of silica. They are found worldwide and are the most common of all the gem species, comprising the greatest and most diverse range of color and form in hard gem materials. Quartz gems are grouped into two types. The first is the visibly crystalline group, which includes amethyst, citrine, rock crystal, and smoky quartz; the second group comprises gems made of microscopically small crystalline aggregates which are found in a large range of colors and patterns and are either translucent or opaque.

The best-known varieties of transparent quartz are rock crystal, a colorless quartz; citrine, which can be yellow or golden or light brown; ametrine, a material that is part amethyst and part citrine; amethyst, lilac to dark purple; smoky quartz, dark brown to smoky brown; and milky quartz, a milky opalescent stone. Opaque varieties are referred to as jasper. Translucent quartz stones are referred to as chalcedony. Red or orange chalcedony is usually called carnelian. Banded varieties of chalcedony are known as agate. When pieces with straight bands are cut from agate boulders, they are known as onyx. White and brown or white and orange colorations are known as sard-onyx. Bright green varieties of chalcedony are known as chrysoprase.

Throughout the ages, rock crystal has perhaps been the gem material most often used in hardstone carving. The word "crystal" comes from the Greek word *krystallos*, meaning ice, because the ancient Greeks thought that the transparent rock crystals were frozen water that had solidified into stone. It is found in large blocks suitable for carving such items as spheres, figures of all sizes, and utilitarian objects. Its frosty surface appeals to our aesthetic sensibilities, inviting tactile as well as visual enjoyment.

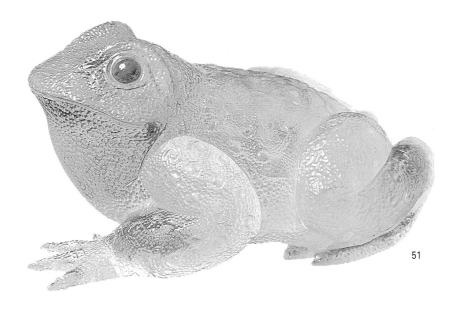

51

54

The clearness and transparent qualities of rock crystal are just the characteristics that appeal to a gem carver, who can use them to advantage on surfaces to which he can give polished or frosted finishes for different effects. Polished rock crystal is transparent but, after details are carved onto its surface, it becomes translucent. Von Zadora-Gerlof is a master at manipulating rock-crystal surface treatment to accentuate the creatures' personality traits, making them appear animated or serene, fanciful or serious.

Two pieces portraying one of the artist's favorite creatures, the frog, illustrate his use of rock crystal. He captures the large frog (fig. 51) in a typically serene yet alert stance. The smaller Frog King whimsically holds court from his perch on a toadstool consisting of a green-enameled mushroom cap supported by a rutilated smoky quartz stem (fig. 42). The base of this sculpture, carved to a matte finish that renders it opaque, further illustrates the versatility of rock crystal. In both sculptures, the creatures are finished to appear much like real ones; however, the sculptor has taken some liberties with the treatment of the skin, carving warts to give the rock crystal more brilliance.

Feathered creatures also lend themselves naturally to depiction in rock crystal. The clear surface allows the sculpting of minutely carved feathers that are more visible in this material than in many other gemstones. Also, the colorless quality of rock crystal can be naturally accented with other colored gem material. Von Zadora-Gerlof's birds can be regal, sweet, intimidating, or arrogant. On most of his rock crystal birds, legs and talons are rendered in gold and seem so real that one would think the actual body part had been dipped in gold.

On the Leghorn rooster (fig. 52), von Zadora-Gerlof replicated the actual white color of the fowl with the comb and wattle in pink tourmaline and an opal for the cheek detail. Just as the feathers in the tail of a rooster are never perfectly smooth, he has added a few gold feathers to depict the rooster ruffling its feathers to impress the hen. The rock crystal

53. Three fledgling birds, 1997. Rock crystal, carnelian, cabochon yellow sapphires, 18-karat gold, agate geode base; height: 4". The fledgling birds are perched in three different stances, watchful and waiting.

54. Swan, 1998. Rock crystal, watermelon tourmaline, yellow diamonds, 18-karat gold; height: 2 1/2", length: 6". Elegance and refinement epitomize both the pose and the attention to detail on this swan.

Following pages

55. Snowy owls, 1998. Rock crystal, cabochon tsavorites, 18-karat gold, green-tinged rock-crystal base; length: 8".

56. Falcon, 1997. Rock crystal, citrine, 18-karat gold, sterling silver, stream-polished agate base; height: 22". The falcon is depicted with its wings outstretched as if having just alighted onto the falconer's glove.

57. Falcon, 1997. Citrine, Malay garnets, 18-karat gold, stream-polished agate base; height: 20".

57

58. Rooster table centerpiece, 1991. Citrine, red tourmaline, 18-karat gold, sodalite base; height: 9 1/2".
Following pages
59. Pair of roosters, 1997. Citrine, red and yellow tourmalines, diamonds, 18-karat gold, British Columbian jadeite base; height: 16 1/2". Both roosters were sculpted from a single citrine crystal that weighed approximately 120 pounds. The stone itself determined the roosters' stance.

body is finished with detailing and without a high polish so that it is less transparent in contrast to the highly polished rock crystal base on which it stands.

In contrast to the feisty rooster the swan (fig. 54) is portrayed as if gliding through water, its slightly raised wings serving as a tiller as it wends its way in the water. Every feather of this graceful swan is artfully depicted for realism: for example, the stiff wing and back feathers are smooth, giving the impression that rain would run off the bird's back. The beak is rendered in a watermelon tourmaline.

Von Zadora-Gerlof also sculpts rock crystal birds in groups, perched and watchful. On one (fig. 53), three fledgling birds sit on the edge of an agate geode nest. Each is in a different pose, but all have their carnelian beaks open, chirping for the worm that, they hope, is on the way. On another group (fig. 57) the white frosted stone replicates the natural coloration of two snowy owls. Von Zadora-Gerlof has sculpted the two mounted atop green-tinged rock crystal in a manner that closely simulates their usual stance in the wild. When hunting, snowy owls perch near the ground in open country, watching for prey. Since the eyes of owls are immovable, they have a unique neck-twisting ability such that they can turn their heads through an arc of 270 degrees. One owl in this group seems to be about to spin his head, looking in another direction for its prey.

Perhaps the most spectacular of von Zadora-Gerlof's rock crystal sculptures is the falcon, which is perched atop a sterling silver falconer's glove and mounted on a stream-polished agate base (fig. 55). Falcons are slender, streamlined birds with long, pointed wings and notched bills. They are exceptionally fast fliers. The gyrfalcon is the largest of the family. It has a variable plumage with coloration ranging from pure white, as in this sculpture, to all black except for white streaking on its underparts. Traditionally, falconry was a sport of the nobility and, in many lands, a man's social status determined which falcon he might own. In Europe, for example, gyrfalcons could be owned only by nobility. In the field, the falcon is carried on the falconer's fist, held by a leather jesse attached to each leg and a leather leash, which the falconer detaches when releasing the falcon to hunt wild quarry.

Von Zadora-Gerlof depicted the rock crystal gyrfalcon with its wings outstretched, having just landed on the falconer's glove. He has attached a bell to the falcon's leg, a device the falconer uses to locate his bird. With its spread wings and extended tail feathers, it is a regal bird, and the artistic pinnacle of the glyptic arts. Von Zadora-Gerlof has made several versions of the falcon in agate, amethyst, labradorite, and one in citrine on an 18-karat gold glove (fig. 56). For this latter sculpture, instead of portraying a bird in action, he presents it perched on the falconer's glove, peering into the distance, looking for his prey.

Citrine lends itself naturally to gemstone carving. It is available in large blocks suitable for sculptures and it ranges in hues from yellow to golden to light brown and is appropriate for many animals. Also, its even distribution of color makes it an easy stone to utilize for a variety of designs. Next to rock crystal, it is the stone von Zadora-Gerlof most often uses in carving. Most of his best specimens come from Minas Gerais, but citrine is also probably the most abundant of all the stones found in the United States.

The rooster table centerpiece (fig. 58) is rendered in a different manner than the previous rock crystal example. Instead of showing a feisty rooster, von Zadora-Gerlof sculpt-

ed this one in a watchful mode. This rooster was commissioned by a client who provided sketches of colorful fowl running wild near the beach on the island of St. Barthélemy. Red tourmaline comb and wattle complete the piece. Von Zadora-Gerlof used a similar material for a pair of roosters, each standing on a base of British Columbian jade (fig. 59). In this sculpture, each rooster stands in a different pose and, if viewed from a certain angle, they appear to be eyeing each other.

In contrast to the stately roosters, the rabbit appears meek and timid (fig. 61). It holds an enameled carrot between its paws, ready to take a bite, but its ears are slightly cocked back, listening for an approaching predator. The body of the rabbit is translucent while the thinner ears are transparent.

A mother kangaroo with her baby in her pouch (fig. 60) is similar to the figure atop the "Delacorte" clock (figs. 26-29). The mother plays a French horn and the baby, a cornet. For this sculpture, von Zadora-Gerlof used the denser, darker part of the stone for the mother's body and head in contrast to the outside of the stone, where the mass is less and the stone is paler and more translucent, for her ears, paws, feet, and tail, as well as the head of the baby. Further variation in this stone is evident in the darker base.

Citrine is an especially suitable stone for a lion sculpture because its brown tones match the natural coloration of the lion's. Von Zadora-Gerlof depicts the king of the jungle in a royal manner. For a centerpiece (fig. 63) heraldic lions hold shields engraved with their owner's coat of arms. Although the fur of lions in the wild tends to be disheveled, the fur on this pair seems to have just been combed, with every piece in place, and their claws appear perfectly manicured, as befits such a regal pair.

Smoky quartz, as the name implies, has a smoky color that varies in intensity from pale brown to nearly black. A hermit crab (fig. 62) is carved from a medium-brown smoky

61

60. Kangaroo with baby in pouch, 1996. Citrine, diamonds, 18-karat gold, citrine base; height: 5". This mother and baby kangaroo sculpture was a study for a similar animal group atop the "Delacorte" clock.

61. Rabbit, 1996. Citrine, cabochon orange sapphires, translucent orange and green enamel, 18-karat gold; height: 3 1/2".

62. Hermit crab, 1990. Rutilated smoky quartz, green tourmaline, 18-karat gold, rock-crystal base; length: 12 1/2".

62

65

Previous pages
63. Heraldic lion centerpiece, 1994. Citrine, 18-karat gold, citrine base; height: 18". Each lion holds a shield with the owner's coat of arms engraved onto the surface in a manner similar to crest engraving on rings.
64. Squirrel Tree, 1987. Citrine, tsavorites, green tourmaline, 18-karat gold, rock-crystal base; height: 8 1/2".
65. Preliminary sketch by Monica von Zadora-Gerlof for Squirrel Tree, 1987. Ink on paper.
66. Frog, 1992. Watermelon tourmaline, canary diamonds, 18-karat gold; length: 2".

quartz, crawling across a rock crystal base. In the species of hermit crabs, the male has one large claw, which it waves in what has been assumed to be a greeting manner, and one smaller claw, which it uses to pick up food. On this sculpture the hermit crab seems to be waving its left claw, perhaps to another crab. Von Zadora-Gerlof has positioned the gold antennae at sharp angles to the crab's body, in stark contrast to the carved stone.

Among the most charming of von Zadora-Gerlof's works are his creature groups depicting several animals, birds, or insects in their natural environment. In many of these groupings trees play a major role, serving as a focal point around which the animals perform their normal functions. On the Squirrel Tree (figs. 64, 65) one squirrel is poised at the top of the tree and watches its companion prepare to bite into a nut. The 18-karat-gold tree is powerfully staged, its thick knar bisecting the scene, forming two different tableaux, with the gaze of the uppermost squirrel serving to tie the two together. At the request of the client who ordered this group, the species of squirrels portrayed here is of a European variety. The design also brought to the artist's mind the squirrels he had encountered in his childhood on the Queen Charlotte Islands. Light brown to golden citrine artfully captures the coloration of each squirrel.

Tourmaline is another transparent stone that von Zadora-Gerlof favors for his work. This stone can produce a wide variety of colors that surpass other gem materials in their versatility. It is found throughout the world, from the Ural Mountains in Russia and Minas Gerais in Brazil to the islands of Madagascar and Ceylon, and in California and Maine in the United States. Tourmaline crystals are often bi-colored, which means that the two ends of a crystal can exhibit completely different hues. One half of a stone may be pink while the other half is green. These stones are also known as watermelon tourmalines. Tourmalines exhibit a directional property known as dichroism whereby the color and clarity of a crystal may vary according to the direction in which it is viewed. When seen from one direction, the stone may be transparent while, from another, no light will shine through it. The gem carver must be aware of this characteristic in order to get optimum results when carving this stone.

66

67. Hummingbird Tree, 1989.
Green tourmaline, watermelon
tourmaline, canary diamonds,
18-karat gold, rock-crystal base;
height: 8".
68. Parrot Tree, 1988. Green
tourmaline, watermelon tourmaline
canary diamonds, cabochon rubies,
18-karat gold, rock-crystal base;
height: 8".

68

70

69. Bird Tree, 1990. Green, red, and pink tourmaline, watermelon tourmaline, citrine, rutilated smoky quartz, canary and pink diamonds, 18-karat gold, base of rock crystal; height: 5 1/2".
70. Preliminary sketch by Monica von Zadora-Gerlof for Bird Tree, 1990. Ink on paper.

Von Zadora-Gerlof prefers tourmalines from Maine for his sculptures. He utilizes the stone's unique bi-color characteristics to advantage on a frog that is only two inches in length (fig. 66). The body and part of the frog's right front and rear legs are pink while the toes, the head, and the other two legs are green. On the Hummingbird Tree sculptural group (fig. 67), von Zadora-Gerlof has carved the birds, orchids, and leaves from this gemstone. For birds and orchids, he chose watermelon tourmalines, but the leaves were executed in the more traditional green hue. One orchid with a gold stem and two leaves can be detached from this group and worn as a brooch.

On the Bird Tree (fig. 69, 70) the leaves are carved out of watermelon tourmaline while one parent bird is sculpted from green tourmaline and the other from pink tourmaline. Each of the three babies in the rutilated smoky quartz nest are carved from a different stone: one from green tourmaline, one from pink tourmaline, and the third from citrine. Like all his sculptural groups, the composition of this Bird Tree has been thoughtfully staged. One parent bird perches on a high branch while the other sits on a lower branch with the nest of fledglings between them. They look as if they are guarding their offspring against potential harm.

The pink and green coloration on the two parrots in the Parrot Tree (fig. 68) sculptural group is very closely matched because von Zadora-Gerlof carved the pair from the same piece of watermelon tourmaline. As with the Hummingbird Tree, he has selected green tourmaline for the leaves but in a paler shade that is more in keeping with an exotic tree. The denseness of the leaves and vines winding around the branch give the feeling of the Amazonian jungle that these two parrots call home.

The "Frog Apple" (fig. 71, 72) was inspired by a visit the artist made to New York, which is often called the Big Apple. At first he was overwhelmed by the vastness of the city, but once he stepped into his client's apartment and its terrace garden, he felt the calmness and serenity of being high above the bustling world, similar to what he imagined a frog would feel on its lily pad. Inspired by this experience, he created a see-through rock crystal apple with contrasting tourmaline frogs, each in a different color. The apple opens to reveal a frog sitting on a gold waterlily leaf in the pond. (This frog can also be worn as a brooch.) When closed, one frog sits atop the lid while another peeps out of a semi-circular hole on the side. From the gold stem grows a watermelon tourmaline leaf.

Opaque varieties of quartz are known as jasper. This is a granular, compact stone, usually containing many impurities that cause the material to be mottled in colors of dark red, brown, yellow, green or gray. Von Zadora-Gerlof uses these deviations to good advantage in much the same way he does with transparent stones. The poppy jasper that makes up the body of the chick (fig. 73) is colored in reddish brown, yellow, and white. The chick has just emerged from the egg in which he stands. The splashes of white on its body are bits of the shell still adhering to its feathers. The artist completes the jasper scheme by using yellow jasper for the beak.

Chalcedony is a translucent variety of the quartz family. It can be cut and polished to a high luster and has been used in jewelry and ornamental carvings throughout history.

71, 72. Frog Apple, 1982. Rock crystal, green tourmaline, watermelon tourmaline, yellow diamonds, 18-karat gold; height: 5", diameter: 4". Two views of Frog Apple, one open and the other closed.

71

73

73. Chick, 1990. Poppy and yellow jasper, diamonds, 18-karat gold, sterling silver; height: 4". The poppy jasper was mined in Morgan Hill, California.

Agate is a banded variety of chalcedony, made up of nodular masses, and consists of one or more varieties of quartz, which gives it interesting colors and patterns. Their interior configurations are essentially striped and can vary in color and width from one piece to another. The stripes can run parallel to each other, follow a zig-zag pattern, or go in a straight line, usually in a concentric configuration. Agates tend to be pale in color, with the most common shades in milky white, yellow, red, and brown, while blues and greens are the rarest. Every agate is unique, there are no two stones that are exactly alike. For this reason, this gem material has been a favorite with carvers since it allows them an infinite number of possibilities to create original pieces.

Von Zadora-Gerlof has created a rhinoceros out of agate with thick skin and one horn on its snout (fig. 75) inspired by Albrecht Dürer's famous engraving of the subject. Like the Dürer print, this sculpture has more "armor" on its body than a real rhinoceros, probably a popular misconception from Dürer's time.

Carved hardstones lend themselves naturally to sculptures of household pets. The three long-haired dachshunds (fig. 77) carved in gray-and-brown striped agate were requested by a client. Each measures five inches in length and, together, the trio makes a stunning sculptural group. The hand-painted rock crystal eyes add a life-like touch to the dogs. Red enamel collars add a dash of color to the gray-brown tones.

Von Zadora-Gerlof created a buffalo out of a brownish agate with gray agate horns (fig. 74). The figure is based on the European bison, which has a larger head than its American counterpart. Like the real beast, it has been portrayed with the distinctive hump on its back extending over its shoulders just back of the neck, and tapering gradually back to the hips.

Sometimes von Zadora-Gerlof combines two different stones within a piece. Such is the case with the bowl (fig. 78) carved from a piece of multi-colored agate with a poppy jasper toad inside. The two stones complement each other with the yellowish and reddish tones of the agate reiterated in the poppy jasper. The sculptor has caught the road about to leap out of the bowl with its feet placed on the rim and its back legs ready to propel it out. This is a whimsical piece, one to be enjoyed just for the pleasure of looking at it.

In contrast to the action of the frog, the artist has sculpted a gentle fawn (fig. 76) out of honey-brown agate in a hue similar to a real deer. Like the young animal itself, von Zadora-Gerlof has made its legs long and gangling but, instead of depicting the fawn standing, he has chosen a moment when the animal is resting, one of its long legs stretched out in front of its body. It appears calm and serene, not yet aware of the dangers it will face in the forest. Von Zadora-Gerlof has utilized the stone to its sculptural potential with the darker, center part of the agate as the body and the outer, lighter section for leg, ears and nose.

Since every piece of agate is different, every sculpture in this gem material is unique in coloration. Von Zadora-Gerlof selected a banded variety in brown and white tones for the body of a sandpiper (fig. 79) in which its back is striped, simulating its mottled feathers, while its underside is white. The egg-shaped body sits on long, spindly gold legs, giving the impression that the bird is about to quickly run away. It stands atop an agate crust base, set with diamonds for the organisms that wash up on the beach, providing food for the bird.

Taking a cue from the dramatic and regal falcons discussed above, the artist created an equally spectacular eagle in the act of snatching a fish out of the water (fig. 80). Honey-colored agate gives just the right tonality for the bird's majestic body and outstretched wings, while white jade provides a realistic match for its head and tail feathers. The aggressive eagle has been executed in a darker stone in contrast to its stricken prey by using a lighter-toned gray agate for the fish, choppy water, and base, setting up a foil between the hunter and the hunted.

Of all opaque gemstones, jade is perhaps the most popular for jewelry and carvings. The name of this stone applies to two varieties of minerals, nephrite and jadeite. The color of nephrite depends on the amount of iron oxide in the mineral and can range from near white to dark green. Jadeite is a silicate of sodium and aluminum with some traces of other metals. It is rarer than nephrite and, of the two jades, the more highly sought after. Colors of jadeite include white, pale blue, orange, red, mauve, violet, yellow, and, of

74. Buffalo, 1998. Brown and grey agate, hand-painted rock crystal, agate base; length: 6 1/2".
Following pages
75. Rhinoceros, 1997. Grey agate, garnets; height: 7", length: 10". The rhinoceros's stance is based on Albrecht Dürer's famous engraving of the animal.

74

76. Fawn, 1998. Honey-brown
agate, black jade, citrine base;
height: 4″.

77. Trio of long-haired dachshunds, 1988. Grey and brown agate, hand-painted rock crystal, red enamel, 18-karat gold; length: 5".

78. Toad in bowl, 1987. Poppy jasper, agate, hand-painted rock crystal, length: 8". The toad is struggling to get out of an unusually striated and colored agate bowl.

79. Sandpiper, 1998. Banded agate, cabochon sapphires, diamonds, 18-karat gold, agate geode base; height: 6". This sandpiper is a study for a sculptural group of three birds running along the beach.

80. Eagle, 1998. Honey-colored and grey agate, white jadeite, garnets, cabochon citrine, 18-karat gold, agate base; height: 19". The eagle sculpture epitomizes the artist's skill as a gemstone carver as well as his unerring eye for selecting suitable stones to capture the essence of his subject.

course, green. The greens range from greenish white and apple green to the most highly prized, emerald green. Jade has been used for carved ornamental objects for several centuries, especially in China, where it is treasured for its beauty.

Jade is a compact and fibrous hardstone, which makes it a very tough material. For this reason, cutting and carving it is very difficult. In China artists and artisans have maintained expertise in carving the stone over many centuries; in contrast, very few Western carvers have undertaken the arduous task of sculpting this material. Only after much trial and error was von Zadora-Gerlof able to master this stone. He now enjoys working with it and looks forward to the challenges that undoubtedly will face him with every new sculpture.

Although he works mostly with green tones of nephrite and jadeite, he did sculpt a monkey (fig. 82) out of black jade early in his career. The client for this piece, a jeweler, sketched the initial design idea for the monkey on the back of a matchbook. Von Zadora-Gerlof sculpted the amusing pose of the seated animal with its paws in back of its ears as if to hear better. For color contrast and to denote the area that is not covered with fur on the animal, he made the face and ears out of brown agate. The monkey sits next to an 18-karat-gold palm tree.

79

Other early commissions include a Tyrannosaurus Rex (fig. 81) and a crocodile (fig. 83), both sculpted out of green jade. When von Zadora-Gerlof created the Tyrannosaurus Rex, he researched the literature available at the time in order to make the reptile as close to the actual creature as possible. Alas, new information has rendered this earlier knowledge out of date. Nevertheless, both reptiles are fierce and menacing, their mouths lined with rhodochrosite and their jaws filled with threatening teeth.

Common pond frogs are green, so it seems a natural choice to carve them in jade. For a group of musical frogs (fig. 84) von Zadora-Gerlof selected a piece of nephrite from British Columbia from which he carved all the figures, thus ensuring an even color distribution in every frog. Like the bronze musical frog group (fig. 8), he borrowed elements from several species of frogs for these figures. The protruding bellies came from the bullfrog or jungle frog, while his inspiration for the hands, feet, and heads was the tree frog. The five musicians sit astride brown agate toadstools, playing 18-karat gold instruments with guilloche and transparent enamel detailing. The conductor waves his 18-karat gold baton. He is the only figure with his mouth open, perhaps quietly singing the song he is conducting.

British Columbian nephrite was also the gem material of choice for a Jackson chameleon (fig. 85). (Von Zadora-Gerlof has also sculpted another, much larger one.) This lizard is known for its ability to change the color of its skin to adapt to whatever environment it finds itself in and avoid detection by its enemies. It is also known for its projectile tongue, which quickly darts out of its mouth to seize its nearby prey. In this piece, this unusual tongue is sculpted out of carnelian with the coiled end reiterating the same shape at the end of its tail. The chameleon sits not on another gemstone but on a piece of petrified wood.

A personal favorite of this author's is the javelina wild boar (fig. 86), which is also made out of British Columbian nephrite. Every part of its body has been replicated exactly down to the hoof protrusion. When touching the sculpture, one can feel the tendons, muscles, sinews and bones underneath the animal's fur. To accomplish this, von Zadora-Gerlof carved

82

81. Tyrannosaurus Rex, 1985. Jadeite, quartz, rhodochrosite, hand-painted rock crystal; height: 9 1/2".

82. Monkey, 1986. Black jade, brown agate, white and colored diamonds, 18-karat gold; height: 2 1/2".

83. Crocodile, 1985. Jadeite, quartz, rhodochrosite, hand-painted rock crystal; length: 18 1/2". The Tyrannosaurus rex, monkey, and crocodile sculptures were commissioned by the same client.

83

85

Previous pages
Frog musicians, 1998. British
Columbian nephrite, brown agate,
cabochon rubies, 18-karat gold,
guilloche with yellow, blue, green,
red transparent enamel; average
height of figures: 5". These figures
are the prototypes for the bronze
frog musicians (see fig. 8).
85. Jackson chameleon, 1998.
British Columbian nephrite,
carnelian, diamonds, 18-karat gold,
petrified wood base; height:
11 1/2". The idea for this figure
came from the artist's daughter,
who had a Jackson chameleon
as a pet.

the body in approximately ninety to a hundred different planes. The boar sculpture took nearly a month to complete, with four to five days to "rough" the shape from the stone, two to two-and-a-half weeks to carve the figure, and another several days to polish it. He has truly captured the essence of the boar, depicting the beast striding with its right hind leg behind and its mighty head raised as if about to snort. This piece was commissioned by the late Michael von Clemm for the oldest and most prestigious of the exclusive final clubs at Harvard University, the Porcelian Club, whose membership has included such notables as Theodore Roosevelt. The mascot for this club is the boar.

The feldspar group of minerals includes moonstone, amazonite, sunstone, and labradorite. The base mineral for each of these stones is silicate of aluminum, to which impurities of either sodium, potassium, or calcium are added. Labradorite or Labrador stone was originally found along the coasts of Labrador. Today, deposits are mined in Australia, Madagascar, Mexico, Russia, and the United States. Although normally a greyish-blue opaque stone, flashes of red, green, and yellow can be seen when the stone is turned. This play of colors determines the quality of these stones; broad flashes, especially in peacock blues, are the most desirable. Endowed with this unusual coloration spectrum, this stone could not but appeal to von Zadora-Gerlof, who prefers gem material with unique, distinctive characteristics. For example, every piece of labradorite radiates different colored hues, giving each one an individual personality.

Von Zadora-Gerlof has used labradorite to good advantage to replicate the actual fur or feathers of certain animals and birds. On a turkey sculpture (fig. 89), for example, blue and yellow splashes highlight the tips of the wings, while the grayish part of the stone makes up the body and tail feathers. Chalcedony and carnelian for the head and neck and a tiger eye beak accent the turkey as it sits atop a jasper base.

In a smaller piece, a labradorite barn owl (fig. 87) sits atop a sterling silver stump, watching for its prey. This species of owl is a cosmopolitan bird, living in many parts of the world. It is a keen hunter with acute hearing that enables it to hear even the faintest sounds, such as a soft rustling of leaves. Von Zadora-Gerlof designed this owl with an 18-karat gold hooked beak and strong curved claws, poised as if listening for the sound of a scurrying rodent. He captured it in a different pose vis-à-vis the two rock crystal snowy owls (fig. 57). On the latter, both are perched near the ground, while the barn owl is sitting higher up, on a stump. The artist sculpted each species of owl in a material suitable to its color, rock crystal for the snowy owl and labradorite for the barn owl. The barn owl sculpture was donated to the ASPCA, where it was sold at auction. It seems fitting that one of von Zadora-Gerlof's sculpted creatures should benefit such a deserving, animal-oriented charity.

Labradorite is also a natural color for the gray fur of two mice (fig. 88). Von Zadora-Gerlof selected different specimens of the stone for each mouse: one is grayer; the other has splashes of blue. The bodies of each mouse are carved to resemble the actual animals, with particular attention to delineating every detail of their fur. The mice are captured in the perfectly natural act of eating cheese: one nibbles on a slice while the other sniffs its partly eaten piece.

Spectrolite is the trade name for labradorite from Finland, a hardstone that exhibits fine spectral colors. Von Zadora-Gerlof created one sculpture out of this material, a sailfish (fig. 91) that was commissioned by a client who loves the open sea. The artist placed the sailfish in the center of two highly polished, rock crystal waves that seem to curl up, ready to snatch the fish out of the air and return it to its natural habitat. This design of the turbulent wave motif is based on Japanese art.

Because of the play of color in labradorite, it is occasionally confused with opal, a gem also characterized by its display of flashes of color. Opal is very different from other gemstones and is one that very few gem carvers use in their work. (Another artist who also works in opal, and whom von Zadora-Gerlof admires, is Thomas McPhee, also from British Columbia.) It is made up of silica and a varying amount of water, ranging from six to ten percent. The remarkable play of colors stems from an internal structure that is amorphous rather than crystalline. For von Zadora-Gerlof, opal offers an endless variety of colors that he uses to great advantage on pieces such as the kingfisher (fig. 90). By combining several different colors of opal and fitting them together seamlessly, he created a sculpture that appears painted rather than put together with gemstones. He chose a blue-gray opal for the bird's back, reddish-orange for the breast, white for the throat and other details, and a grayish opal for the beak. The fish in his beak is carved from a reddish-orange opal. The kingfisher stands on a quartz mineral base.

After this review of von Zadora-Gerlof's hardstone animal figures, it is appropriate to sketch a brief comparison with those made in Fabergé's workshop at the turn of the century. Clearly, both artists draw upon similar animals, birds, and amphibians for inspiration, including the mouse, monkey, bison, rhinoceros, dog, owl, rooster, frog, and

86. Javelina wild boar, 1997. British Columbian nephrite, white jade, cabochon rubies, 18-karat gold; height: 8", length: 15". The fur on this boar has been finished in such detail that it appears as bristly as that of the actual animal.

86

87. Barn owl, 1995.
Labradorite, cabochon
tsavorites, 18-karat gold,
sterling silver base;
height: 7".
89. Turkey, 1988.
Labradorite, chalcedony,
carnelian, tiger eye,
diamonds, 18-karat gold,
jasper base; height: 6".

87

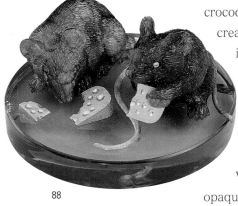

88

88. Mice with cheese, 1997. Labradorite, platinum, diamonds, 18-karat gold, citrine base; diameter: 2 3/4". This group was a study for the mouse clocks (see figs. 119, 120).

90. Kingfisher, 1987. Opals, hand-painted rock crystal, silver vermeil, quartz mineral base; height: 3". The iridescence of the kingfisher's feathers suggested the use of opal for this sculpture.

91. Sailfish, 1990. Spectrolite, diamonds, 18-karat gold, polished rock crystal base; height: 12 1/2". The sailfish is part of a series of six creatures that also includes a dolphin, shark, lobster, hermit crab, and Dungeness crab.

crocodile, to name only a few. Also, both succeeded in capturing the personality of each creature within a block of stone. Fabergé employed technically proficient carvers to implement his designs, most of which are less than three inches in height. Von Zadora-Gerlof has personally sculpted his figures and in a much broader range of sizes and gem varieties. Fabergé's creatures, for the most part, exhibit very little movement, often appearing as if posing for a portrait. In contrast, von Zadora-Gerlof's are animated creations of animals, birds, or amphibians, seemingly caught in the act of living a moment of their natural lives.

Von Zadora-Gerlof has certainly defied normal boundaries in his translucent and opaque sculptures inspired by the animal kingdom. On each piece he has carefully matched the creature to be carved with the most appropriate gem material, often searching for a long time for the right match. He is a perfectionist not only in his selection of gemstones but also in his exacting attention to even the smallest details.

90

CHAPTER 3

OBJECTS FOR THE HOME AND OFFICE

The inherent beauty of hardstones has always made them a natural choice for enhancing the aesthetic appeal of functional items. Since gems are relatively scarce, as are the specialized skills required for their utilization, wealth and social status have increasingly been associated with possession of gem-enhanced objects. The history of this branch of the glyptic arts dates back to the third century B.C. when a center was established at Alexandria for carving hardstone vessels. By 200 B.C., artisans working in Rome created monolithic vessels in rock crystal and agate. During the Medieval and Renaissance periods, antique vessels were incorporated into silver-gilt mountings, and, by the mid sixteenth century, hardstone carving had become an established art form with gifted artists creating elaborate vessels with richly embellished surfaces. Fabergé continued this tradition in Russia at the turn of the century, designing beautiful functional objects using hardstones with gold and precious and semi-precious stones for accent.

Over the past twenty years, Andreas von Zadora-Gerlof has become the leading artist in this branch of the glyptic arts, devoting to it the same inspiration and attention to detail in design and craftsmanship that he brought to the other areas of his oeuvre. As with his purely decorative works, these functional sculptures rival those magnificent pieces made by the great hardstone carvers throughout history.

Although the art of sculpting functional objects is not fundamentally different from that of sculpting ornamental objects, the artist must be aware of some additional considerations. Functional objects, by their very nature, are meant to be used—to be picked up and handled, rather than placed on a shelf or in a cabinet. Thus, it is important to select stones that not only feel nice to the touch but also provide a different dimension of light and shadow. Of course, a critical consideration must be that all the gem material used for these objects be durable enough to withstand many, many years of use.

92. Cup, 1997. Rhodonite, sterling silver, green enamel, cabochon rubies, diamonds, 18-karat gold, black jasper base; height: 8 1/2". The artist selected this particular rhodonite because, in his words, "The stone looked fantastic!"

93. Fish salt cellars, 1990. Aquamarine, cabochon pink tourmalines, 18-karat gold, mineral base; length: 3 3/4".

93

95

Previous pages
94. Snail place-card holders, 1998.
Citrine, aquamarine, red and blue
tourmaline, watermelon tourmaline,
diamonds, 18-karat gold;
height: 3/4".
95. Lion place-card holder and salt
and pepper shakers, 1994. Citrine,
guilloche with transparent red
enamel, 18-karat gold; height
of place-card holder: 3 3/4", height
of salt and pepper shakers: 2 1/4".
The place-card holder and salt and
pepper shakers are part of a set of
twelve that were designed along
with the heraldic lion centerpiece
(see fig. 63).

Von Zadora-Gerlof carefully selects each stone, making sure that it is perfectly suited for a particular piece. For some objects, he prefers transparent gem material such as rock crystal or citrine; for others, he favors opaque stones such as agate or nephrite. His approach is to let each piece tell him which stone to use. Some objects call for light, either natural or artificial, to bounce off their surfaces, creating a luminous play of colors that gives them another dimension. For some objects, he uses ornamental crystals and minerals that are barely known to the general public, such as fluorite or rhodonite.

Hardstones lend themselves admirably to the creation of elegant pieces for use at the dinner table, such as place card holders and containers for condiments. Since these pieces will be set on tables often lit by candlelight, von Zadora-Gerlof polishes the gem material to a high gloss so that light will bounce off the surface, giving a warm radiance to each item. In a very real sense, each piece is meant to be like a jewel at the table, to provide visual interest as well as to offer the service for which it is intended.

His snail place card holders (fig. 94) feature an artful combination of transparent stones for each mollusk. All the bodies are carved from citrine, while aquamarine, red and blue tourmaline, and watermelon tourmaline make up the shells. Eighteen-karat gold eye stalks and feelers, set at their ends with diamonds, are naturalistically depicted on the top of each snail's head. Although the snails are similar in design, close examination reveals that each has its own distinctive features.

One lion place card holder and salt and pepper shaker set (fig. 95) are carved from citrine, and are part of the table service that complements the heraldic lion centerpiece seen earlier (fig. 63). The gemstones used for all pieces of the set exhibit a rich golden brown coloration. On the place card holder, the plume behind the lion passant has a richer golden tonality. Von Zadora-Gerlof continues to play on the regal theme with this set, placing the lion, as the king of the jungle, in front of a plume, the Prince of Wales' insignia.

A client who lives in Vermont and keeps a pond stocked with trout commissioned salt cellars (fig. 93). Since fish tend to be blue toned, von Zadora-Gerlof selected aquamarine to carve the two playful fish with their mouths open, ready to receive the salt. He set each fish atop a bluish mineral base, suggesting the frothy sea, rather than his client's quieter pond, and designed special salt spoons with shell-like bowls.

For the octopus place card holder (fig. 96), he chose a gray agate, similar in color to the actual mollusk. He carved the tentacles with their suckers underneath curling around the edge of the sculpture and polished the surface so that it resembles the skin of the slimy creature. This card holder is one of a series created for a client's yacht, an appropriate setting for this marine animal. On another place card holder (fig. 97), the mottled red, tan, and dark tones of the poppy jasper simulate the shell of a hermit crab sitting atop a rock crystal base that looks like a piece of ice. These carefully rendered pieces are fun to look at, make interesting conversation at the table, and are small works of art that also happen to be useful.

96. Octopus place-card holder, 1990. Grey agate, diamonds, 18-karat gold, rock crystal base; diameter: 3 1/2".
97. Hermit crab place-card holder, 1990. Poppy jasper, orange diamonds, 18-karat gold, rock crystal base; length: 3 1/2". The octopus and hermit crab place-card holders were commissioned by the same client, who enjoys aquatic life.

96

97

98. Bowl, 1996. Fluorite; height: 5 1/2". The unique wide and narrow purple striations provide the only decorative accent on this bowl.
99. Bowl with frog, 1998. Nephrite, cabochon sapphires, 18-karat gold; diameter: 5".

98

Whereas von Zadora-Gerlof often depicts whimsical creatures in his small table articles, his hollowware tends to be more traditional in design. These objects are usually larger in size and tend to play a more permanent role in home or office décor, suggesting a more conventional approach. At the same time, their size may limit the options of gemstone material to be used.

The bowl sculpted out of fluorite with purple striations (fig. 98) is an interesting example of the range of materials he uses. Fluorite, or calcium fluoride, is rarely found in its pure colorless state. With the addition of various impurities as well as structural imperfections, the gem material becomes colored in shades of green, yellow, or purple. Carved by the Romans into bowls, cups, and vases, fluorite has been a popular gem material for carving ornamental objects. Von Zadora-Gerlof selected this particular stone because of its unique stripes, both wide and thin and in varying shades of purple, to provide the only decorative accent. This is the type of gem material that contemporary glass makers try to imitate without ever really succeeding.

On a nephrite bowl (fig. 99), von Zadora-Gerlof accented its stark, pure color by adding a few gold touches. Gold ball feet support the vessel while one of his favorite amphibians, a gold frog, attempts to scramble up the side. This gem material was favored by Fabergé, who also created small bowls out of nephrite.

The cup, as a sculptural form, has been carved in hardstones since the Roman period. It was especially popular with the Medicis who often incorporated vessels from ancient times into contemporary mounts. Von Zadora-Gerlof has captured the spirit of the Renais-

99

sance in this pink rhodonite cup (fig. 92), standing on a black jasper base. Rhodonite is a manganese silicate of extreme hardness, which makes it suitable for ornamental carvings. It has been used for beads as well as small and large carvings. A single slab was used for the sarcophagus of Alexander II of Russia. Also, the Russian building at the 1939 World's Fair in New York had a gigantic map of the country composed of inlaid mineral plates of different colors with the land masses made up of purplish-red rhodonite. On this rhodonite cup, the handles are formed by two green enameled snakes whose bodies twist into a knot-like form. It is a splendid modern version of its ancient antecedents.

Rock crystal has been a natural stone for carving hollowware. Large, flawless quartz crystals were in demand since before Christ as the raw material from which vases, bowls, and goblets were carved. The Romans appreciated its colorless quality and used it to create monolithic vessels. Carving in this material is difficult and can push the patience and endurance of a lapidary to their limits. Before carving can begin, a near-perfect piece of rock crystal must be found. The most desired pieces are those that are only slightly flawed or "veiled"—those that look almost like crystal. After securing the block of rock crystal, the lapidary begins to hollow out the center to bring the walls to the desired thinness without exerting too much pressure in cutting into the stone or it will crack and, possibly, break. The finished object is then polished. Carving hollow vessels in rock crystal is an arduous task that calls for fortitude and stamina.

Von Zadora-Gerlof has created several hollowware pieces in rock crystal, all sculpted from one block of stone. The body of one vase (fig. 100) has been hollowed out of the stone, leaving a sufficient amount of rock crystal at the top to carve the thickened rim and decorative ring just below. The 18-karat gold base, standing atop reeded ball feet, is embellished with white enamel and guilloche with green transparent enamel. Another vase (fig. 101) is almost three times as large. The entire vessel was carved from one piece of rock crystal, including the inverted pyriform body, neck, and base. The fluting on the collar reflects upwards into the plain turned rim, giving an added dimension to the lip. The vase is set into an 18-karat gold stem of guilloche with white opalescent enamel on a domed base.

Von Zadora-Gerlof's tour de force in rock-crystal holloware is the urn (fig. 102) that required not only an exceptionally large piece of quartz but also a fine specimen with very few flaws. It rivals the great vessels from the Medieval and Renaissance periods. Unlike the earlier vessels with their elaborate ornamentation, the design of this urn is quite simple. The globular form is made of a fluted lower section contrasted to an unadorned upper body with a reticulated 18-karat gold band that, visually, ties the two halves together. In actuality, this band only provides support for the textured gold-scrolled handles. The base is a separate piece of rock crystal that is joined to the main body. This urn is truly a superb work of art, fit for a king.

Von Zadora-Gerlof has sculpted candle holders in several gem materials. The pair of candlesticks with fluted shafts (fig. 103) are made out of citrine. Decorative interest is provided with guilloche on the bobeches and rim of the sockets with a wavy design in red transparent enamel repeated on the connecting rings.

100

100. Vase, 1996. Rock crystal, 18-karat gold, white enamel, guilloche with transparent green enamel; height: 5 1/2".
Following pages
101. Vase, 1998. Rock crystal, 18-karat gold, guilloche with opalescent white enamel; height: 14". The rock crystal used to form this vase is almost flawless.
102. Urn, 1998. Rock crystal, 18-karat gold; height: 11 1/2". The artist selected the rock crystal on this urn for its interesting internal inclusions.

103. Candlesticks, 1998. Citrine, 18-karat gold, guilloche with transparent red enamel; height: 9″. The artist has designed other pairs in rock crystal and jadeite.
104. Candelabra, 1998. Wyoming jadeite, 18-karat gold, guilloche with transparent red enamel; height: 12″.

The pair of candelabra in Wyoming jadeite (fig. 104) are more elaborately conceived. Like the candlesticks, the shaft of each candelabrum is fluted. Textured 18-karat gold branches support fluted sockets with guilloche bobeches and rim. Articulated swags are suspended from the branches. Color accent is provided by the guilloche with red transparent enamel rings between the shaft and base.

Whereas the candle holders discussed above are more traditional in design, the mountain sheep ram's head candelabra (fig. 105) are quite unique in their conception. Von Zadora-Gerlof has sculpted two ram's heads of the European species out of rutilated smoky quartz, mounting the silver vermeil bobeches on the ends of the curling horns. Departing from a strict naturalistic portrayal for artistic effect, he sculpted the horns so that their tips twist around as supports for the candle holders. Like in all his animal sculptures, he artfully replicated the thick fur of the ram, detailing every strand.

103

For some of his pieces, von Zadora-Gerlof favors stones with rutiles, which are fine needles of another mineral within the basic stone. Such is the case with the material for the ram's head candelabra as well as for a desk set (fig. 106). Textured 18-karat gold acorns and oak leaves complement the gold rutiles embedded in the smoky quartz. In contrast, he created another desk set (fig. 107) from colorless rock crystal in a quilted design, finished with 18-karat gold bands.

Although von Zadora-Gerlof has not been commissioned to make many desk sets, the two illustrated here are outstanding examples of this decorative art form. Most desk sets are made out of leather or metals such as bronze, copper, or silver. In comparison, the hardstone material used for these two sets lends them a more majestic aura. The gem material is hard enough for the items to be used and enjoyed everyday without worry of chipping or breaking. These desk accessories rival the pieces Fabergé created in such materials as nephrite, embellished with gold and silver mounts.

The rock crystal Frog Prince pen holder (fig. 108) reminds us once again of this artist's love for this creature. Although the skin of real-life frogs is smooth, he purposely makes the body, arms, and legs lumpy. He does this to give the rock crystal more brilliance, to break the light. This pen holder is enchanting and amusing in its design while still fulfilling its intended function.

106

107

107. Desk set comprising blotter ends, magnifying glass, box, letter knife, letter rack and calendar base, 1991. Rock crystal, cabochon rubies, 18-karat gold; length of blotter ends: 12". The design on this set was inspired by Coco Chanel's quilted patternings.
108. Frog Prince pen holder, 1988. Rock crystal, diamonds, sapphires, cabochon rubies, 18-karat gold; height: 4 1/2". The large-mouthed frog seemed a suitable figure to hold pens and an amusing alternative to the usual pen holders.

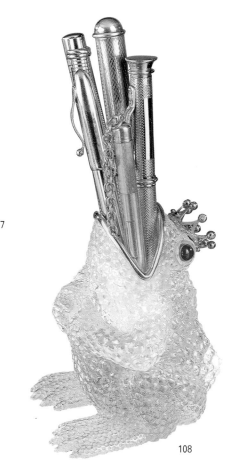

108

Paper knives have been popular since the last quarter of the nineteenth century when elegant implements for the desk became essential accoutrements for the successful businessman. The basic shape, with its elongated blade and long handle, made it an adaptable form on which to etch, engrave, or otherwise apply decorative motifs. Made in a variety of materials including bronze, silver, gold, and ivory, these knives were elevated to an art form by Fabergé, who created paper knives in all types of hardstones. During the art deco period, Cartier offered exquisite gemstone desk accessories in the prevalent rectilinear style with paper knives carved in gem material and, often, a clock in the handle.

Von Zadora-Gerlof has reintroduced these luxurious articles in a variety of gem materials. He has made them either as one piece of a desk set, such as the rutilated smoky quartz and rock crystal examples mentioned above, in which the design matches the other pieces, or as individual works of art. His paper knives have hardstone blades and figural handles, as seen in the lapis lazuli frog joined to a gray agate blade (fig. 110). As in many of his frog sculptures, the warty skin adds tactile enjoyment and surface brilliance. The color palette on this paper knife has been carefully selected so that the deep blue stone of the handle is reiterated in the softer shade of the blade.

Frogs are also the decorative motif on the British Columbian jadeite paper knife, designed to complement the photograph frame (fig. 109). Eighteen-karat, gold-textured

109. Photograph frame and paper knife, 1986. British Columbian jadeite, cabochon rubies, 18-karat gold; height of frame: 4 1/2", length of paper knife: 8". This frame and paper knife were the artist's first attempt at making such items and have remained in his collection.

110. Letter knife, 1986. Lapis lazuli, cabochon emeralds, 18-karat gold, grey agate blade; length: 8". After completing a project with lapis lazuli elements, the artist discovered that the leftover cuttings were suitable for the frog on this paper knife.

109

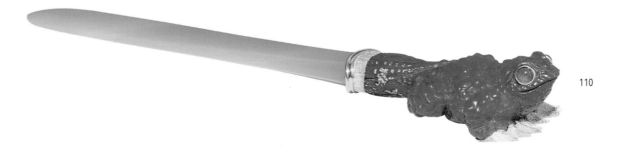

110

climbing tree frogs ornament the handle of the paper knife and the surface of the frame while two other frogs serve as the supporting feet for the frame. The jadeite on the blade of the paper knife and on the photograph frame is a beautiful dark green with black flecks.

Photograph frames have been designed to accent images of loved ones. They are made in a wide range of mediums and prices vary dramatically depending upon the materials used. Traditional frames are normally rectilinear, and any decoration is limited to the area around the picture. Von Zadora-Gerlof created frames that boldly defy the term, becoming more than just a vessel to contain a picture. The glass part of a two-sided photograph frame (fig. 112) is made out of two rock crystal panels that hold the picture in place. The theme of this 18-karat gold frame is aquatic: the bottom side portrays the bottom of the sea and features diamond-set enameled clam and sea snail shells; on the upright, a gem-quality green beryl sea horse is set against a reed, undulating in the water. To add to the functionality of this beautiful object, the sea horse can be detached and worn as a brooch.

The theme of another sculptural photograph frame (fig. 111) is a honeycomb. The material chosen for the frame is citrine, overlaid with an 18-karat gold honeycomb with an attached Queen Bee as the decorative motif. Like the sea horse in the previous frame, this bee can be removed and worn as a piece of jewelry. It features a multi-colored gem-encrusted crown and wings made of watermelon tourmaline with canary diamonds set into its back. Both the Queen Bee and sea horse frames are more than just functional items; they are truly three dimensional objets d'art.

Two sterling silver photograph frames (fig. 116) are designed along more traditional lines. Featuring guilloche with transparent enamel ornamentation, they are reminiscent of similar items from Fabergé's workshop, albeit the latter employed turn-of-the-century styles, embellished with swags and set with pearls or diamonds. Von Zadora-Gerlof provides a simple decoration of enameled lady bugs that, like the sea horse and Queen Bee above, double as wearable pins. These lady bugs subtly contribute another dimension to the flat surfaces of the frames, as well as a counterpoint to their classical geometric lines. They relieve the seriousness of a traditional item, eliciting a smile.

The inspiration for a desk set made out of Wyoming jadeite (fig. 113) came from similar objects designed by the house of Fabergé. Guil-

111

111. Photograph frame with detachable bee brooch, 1991. Citrine, 18-karat gold, watermelon tourmaline, cabochon rubies, canary diamonds, multicolored gemstones; height of frame: 5 1/2".
112. Photograph frame with detachable sea-horse brooch, 1998. Rock crystal, green beryl, diamonds, cabochon rubies, blue and orange enamel, 18-karat gold; height of frame: 5 1/2".

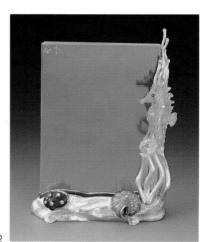

112

114. Door knob, 1996. Nephrite, 18-karat gold; length: 2". This is one of fifty door knobs specially ordered to accessorize the decor on a yacht. This commission was the artist's first attempt to create architectural elements.

115. Pill box, 1981. Falcon's eye, cabochon rubies, yellow sapphire, 18-karat gold; length: 3". This pill box is not only visually appealing, but also invites tactile enjoyment. It was the first such item created by von Zadora-Gerlof.

loche with white opalescent enamel on the dial of the clock, lid of the box, and upper section of the magnifying glass is contrasted to the jadeite, providing a softer accent to the dark green hardstone.

Von Zadora-Gerlof has recently added objects decorated with guilloche with transparent enameling to his repertoire, including kaleidoscopes (fig. 117), an amusing novelty that has always amused both children and adults. The kaleidoscope in guilloche with red transparent enamel is finished on one end with polished rock crystal. The kaleidoscopic images are produced by faceting on the rock crystal that, when turned, creates patterns out of ambient light. The view inside the kaleidoscope with guilloche with royal blue transparent enamel is quite different. When held up to the light, the viewer sees continually changing symmetrical forms made by light passing through faceted gemstones of amethyst, rubies, emeralds, and sapphires suspended in glycerin.

The pill box in the shape of a horse's head (fig. 115) was carved from a rare piece of falcon's eye, a material similar to tiger's eye. Whereas tiger's eye has a gold-brown to gold-yellow coloration, falcon's eye tends toward the darker, almost black hues. The beautiful, subtle stripes of this stone add realism to this sculpted object as seen on the lower part of the horse's head. The artist has accented the piece with an 18-karat gold mane and a clasp set with a yellow sapphire. In conception and size, this pill box is similar to a jasper snuffbox in the guise of a hippopotamus' head made by the house of Fabergé.

114

115

Some of von Zadora-Gerlof's special commissions can be of quite a different character from his nature-inspired creations. One such commission was for fifty door knobs for a client's yacht (fig. 114). Executed in nephrite, these objects are trimmed in 18-karat gold with a lotus pattern band.

Von Zadora-Gerlof has certainly given new meaning to the term "functional." His objects for the home and office go far beyond pure utilitarian use, becoming at times whimsical and at other times quite serious, but always beautiful. Not since the house of Fabergé was creating similar objects have we seen such splendors.

116. Photograph frames with detachable pins, 1996. Sterling silver, 18-karat gold, guilloche with transparent red, blue and yellow enamel; length of frames: 5". These photograph frames represent the artist's interest in making beautiful articles accented with guilloche with transparent enamel.

117. Kaleidoscopes, 1996. 18-karat gold, guilloche with transparent red and blue enamel, opaque white enamel, rock crystal lens; length: 5 1/2".

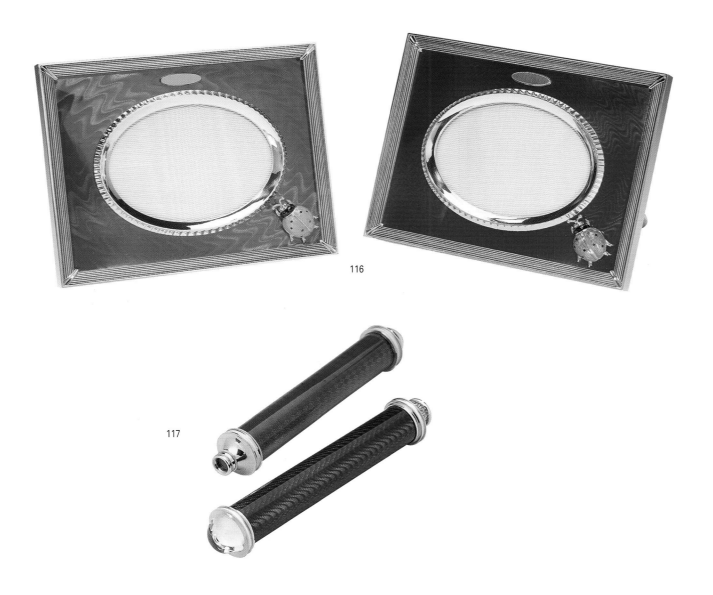

116

117

CHAPTER 4

CLOCKS THAT ALSO TELL TIME

Timekeeping has always occupied the thoughts of man. As civilization progressed, mechanical devices for measuring the hours of the day were developed, but it was not until the fourteenth century that a true mechanical clock was first introduced. At first, the domestic clock was relatively simple, resembling timepieces designed for public spaces. By the seventeenth century, dials were set into pierced silver cases. The following century saw the introduction of dials set into elaborate structures, richly adorned with figures and other ornamentation. Clocks, visual objects by their very function, lend themselves naturally to decoration around the dial face as well as on their casing. Of course, since their use is universal, the desired level of decoration ranges from very ornate to quite plain.

Von Zadora-Gerlof brings to this area of his oeuvre the same degree of imagination and perfection that characterizes his jewelry, desk and table accessories, and sculpture. In fact, his clocks incorporate sculpted figures from the animal and sea world in such a way that telling time takes on a new meaning. In this, he is heir to a great tradition of creating clocks that are much more than just timepieces.

Many great jewelers have created clocks as part of their repertoire, bringing their expertise in the area of precious metals and gemstones to clockmaking, producing timepieces that go beyond purely utilitarian use. Fabergé created gemstone and precious-metal table clocks, enameled and set with pearls and diamonds. They were also celebrated for their Easter eggs, several of which—including the Serpent Clock egg, Bouquet of Lilies Clock egg, the Cockerel egg, and the Colonnade egg—housed timepieces. During the art deco period, Cartier became famous for their mystery clocks, which seemed to mark time with no apparent mechanism. Dials were set into enameled or hardstone mounts in the shapes of screens and porticos but, as elegant and innovative as these models were, it was the *animalia*, or figure subject, mystery clocks for which the house receives international acclaim. For these clocks, Cartier incorporated genuine antique Chinese objects of agate, jade, rock crystal, or coral into the design. Many years later, in

118. Aquatic clock, 1999. Aquamarine, tourmaline, citrine, diamonds, 18-karat gold, guilloche with opalescent white enamel, black enamel, rock crystal base; height: 7".

119

119. Two versions of mouse clock,
1997. Rutilated quartz, labradorite,
diamonds, 18-karat gold, guilloche
with transparent red enamel, agate
plate; height: 4".
120. Rutilated quartz, citrine,
diamonds, 18-karat gold, guilloche
with opalescent white enamel,
jadeite plate; height: 4". The artist
was intrigued with the fun of
depicting mice with more food than
they could imagine (see also the
study in fig. 88).

120

1977, the house reconsidered the popularity of their mystery clocks and offered this line on a special-order basis.

The timepieces that Andreas von Zadora-Gerlof creates follow in this great tradition. With their incorporation of animal forms into the design, they closely follow Cartier's mystery clocks. However, the animal figures that graced Cartier's clocks were Chinese antique pieces, whereas von Zadora-Gerlof's creatures are all sculpted by his own hand. As with all of his special projects, he personally oversees every part of the construction of these elaborate clocks by his work masters, from conception to completion.

Often, von Zadora-Gerlof receives commissions for particular timepieces. Such was the case with the sea horse clock (fig. 122) in which a client requested a timepiece specifically designed for a woman's bedroom. His design consisted of a traditional clock, albeit with diamond-set Roman numerals, placed between two lapis lazuli sea horses atop a rock-crystal clam shell. The colorless base serves as a stage to accentuate the dark blue figures. The sea horses are depicted in a naturalistic manner with dorsal fins, prehensile tails, elongated snouts, and heads bent at right angles to the body. The artist delineated the bodies, emphasizing the bony external plates, and curled their tails, anchoring them to the base. In real underwater life, sea horses use their long, tapering tails to grasp seaweed, fastening themselves to plants.

Von Zadora-Gerlof continued the marine theme on another timepiece in which the design simulates an actual underwater environment (fig. 118). On this piece, he placed a traditional clock face in the center of an asymmetrically-arranged composition featuring a hippocampus on one side and fish on the other, with seaweed connecting them. In Greek mythology, a hippocampus was a sea horse with two equine forelegs and a fish-like body ending in a dolphin tail. Here the hippocampus was designed with a textured 18-

121. Elephant clock, 1996. Gray agate, pearls, diamonds, black jade, guilloche with transparent red and blue enamel, rock crystal base; height: 7 1/2". This clock required the expertise of many workmasters, including a gemstone carver, a goldsmith, an enameler, and a clockmaker.

122. Sea horse clock, 1989. Lapis lazuli, white diamonds, cabochon ruby, 18-karat yellow and white gold, rock crystal base; height: 4".

122

123

karat gold head and neck, shaggy mane, forelegs, and dolphin tail and an aquamarine lower body sculpted with scales. On the opposite side and on top of the clock fish carved from aquamarine, citrine, and tourmaline swim amid seaweed. The entire tableau of sea creatures and plants appears to undulate to the rhythm of the tide. The clock is set on top of a polished rock-crystal base. Its face is artfully finished in guilloche with white opalescent enamel and surrounded by a pavé diamond bezel.

Von Zadora-Gerlof brings to his clock making the same sense of scale and proportion that he brings to his other work. Animals such as the mice on the mouse clocks (figs. 119, 120) are rendered life-size, nibbling on a generous hunk of Swiss cheese. Although from one perspective whimsical, the themes of these clocks are at the same time portrayed realistically; we do envision mice eating cheese. Von Zadora-Gerlof has sculpted the cheese in rutilated quartz in both Mouse clocks variations. On one (fig. 120), the cheese sits on a plate of Wyoming jadeite with dark amber citrine mice; on the other (fig. 119), the plate is agate and the mice are carved from labradorite. The tails of the mice on both clocks are platinum with pavé diamonds. As with all his sculptural groups, he selects gem materials that complement one another in coloration and other features.

On some of von Zadora-Gerlof's sculptural group clocks, he uses large animals to support both the clock and other animals on their backs. Such is the case with the hippopotamus, rhinoceros, and elephant clocks, all featuring large jungle animals. The hippopotamus clock (fig. 124) is designed in a triple strata with the hippopotamus supporting a clock, which in turn supports a baby hippopotamus, the forms becoming smaller as they rise to the top. The composition is arranged in a formal triangular structure, with the larger animal at the base, the clock in the middle, and the smaller animal on the top. To relieve this formality, the artist has introduced a few visual aberrations. The baby hippopotamus not only appears totally disinterested, in fact facing backwards, but is about to lose its balance, while the large, rather ponderous, hippopotamus seems almost too big for the base of rock crystal. Both animals are sculpted from labradorite.

The design of the rhinoceros clock (fig. 125), featuring multiple specimens, is conceived quite differently. Instead of the smaller animal perched on the clock, two oxidized silver monkeys crouch directly on the back of the beast, symmetrically flanking the 18-karat gold-rimmed clock and sharing with it a guilloche-decorated saddle also in 18-karat gold. One arm from each monkey reaches to the top of the clock as if holding it in place while also holding a black enamel spear with platinum shaft. Von Zadora-Gerlof based the body of the rhinoceros on the African species and matched the color of the actual animal in greyish labradorite. It is shown striding on a dark spinach-green nephrite base on which the crossed-spears motif is repeated in gold.

Of the three jungle animal clocks, the elephant (fig. 121) is the only one carrying just a clock. Since elephants are usually gray, von Zadora-Gerlof sculpted the animal in gray agate atop a rock crystal base. The elephant is portrayed with its mouth open and its trunk in the air. The clock is secured to the woven gold saddle by dowel pins with pearls on the end. The saddle is trimmed in guilloche with red transparent enamel, the same enameling as on the dial. The placement of the clock reminds one of a drum on the back of a circus elephant. One can envision the beast carrying its burden as it walks around the circus ring. Von Zadora-Gerlof made another version of this clock with the clock dial of guilloche with white opalescent enamel (fig. 123).

In place of a traditional clock with a horizontal dial facing the viewer, von Zadora-Gerlof has designed some sculptures with orbital dial clocks, sometimes called cylindrical clocks, in which the dial is turned on its side on a cylindrical surface, marking time against a fixed pointer as it rotates. This design keeps the clock mechanism and dial at the bottom, cleanly separated from any ornamentation on top of it, thus giving a sculptor almost unlimited freedom to design the latter.

Von Zadora-Gerlof's obsession with using only the best materials, the best techniques, and an uncompromising attention to detail is extended to his clock maker, David Monroe, who is enlisted to bring accuracy and longevity to these timepieces. In one instance, Monroe suggested that end caps be installed in the orbital dial clocks to reduce friction. According to Monroe, "The inside of the clocks is brought to the same high standards of workmanship as the outside." These clocks are meant to operate for many, many years to come.

The Frog Prince rides on a snail atop an orbital dial clock with black enameled Roman numerals (fig. 126). Monica von Zadora-Gerlof captured the essence of the sculptural group in her sketch (fig. 127), which, along with the finished piece, epitomizes von Zadora-Gerlof's whimsical side as expressed through his favorite creature, the frog, in action. The Frog Prince is executed in a piece of extremely fine green beryl while its mount, the snail, has a citrine body and a red tourmaline shell. As befits his rank, the Frog Prince wears an 18-karat gold crown and sits astride an 18-karat gold saddle, both set with diamonds. Gold accents encircle the snail's shell and serve as the bit and reins. It is a sumptuous piece and, by the way, it also tells time, accurately. Von Zadora-Gerlof liked this theme so much that he also replicated it in bronze for a garden statuary (see fig. 4).

Gemstone-quality green beryl is also used for the hippopotamus standing atop an orbital dial clock (fig. 128). The stance of the animal, standing on its hind legs and playing

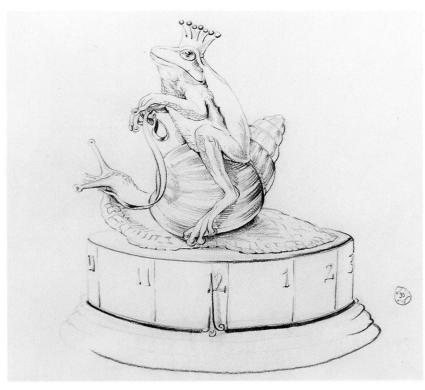

127

126. Frog Prince orbital dial clock, 1996. Green beryl, citrine, red tourmaline, diamonds, cabochon rubies, 18-karat gold, rock crystal base; height: 5". The green beryl and red tourmaline on this clock are gem-facet grade. This clock is the third in this series.
127. Preliminary sketch by Monica von Zadora-Gerlof for Frog Prince orbital dial clock, 1989. Pencil on paper.

128. Hippopotamus orbital dial clock, 1996. Green beryl, 18-karat gold, guilloche with transparent yellow enamel, brown enamel, guilloche with transparent pink enamel, canary diamonds, platinum, rock crystal base; height: 16".
Following pages
129. Bear Tree orbital dial clock, 1997. Yellow amber-colored citrine, tsavorites, 18-karat gold, Kalahari jasper, detachable bee brooches of 18-karat gold, diamonds, cabochon rubies, watermelon tourmaline, rutilated quartz base; height: 14". At the client's request, the artist created a bear in an animated pose, gathering food from a bee's nest. This piece functions on many levels, as a sculpture, a clock, and a receptacle for the jeweled bees.
130. Wasp Tree orbital dial clock, 1988. Sterling silver, 18-karat gold, British Columbian nephrite, 18-karat white and yellow gold, rock crystal base, detachable wasps of 18-karat gold, pearls, guilloche with translucent two-color brown enamel, plique-a-jour enamel, cabochon sapphires; height: 14". The image of the wasp has a special symbolism for the client. The body of each wasp contains a photograph of a member of his family.

a violin, is based on a similar figure on the "Delacorte" clock (see figs. 26-29). Von Zadora-Gerlof has captured the hippopotamus as it positions an 18-karat gold and platinum bow onto an 18-karat gold violin in guilloche with yellow transparent enamel and brown enamel. He made a second version of this clock with the hippopotamus sculpted from citrine and the violin in guilloche with red transparent enamel and black enamel.

Another group that utilizes citrine for the main figure is the Bear Tree (fig. 129), in which the animal is carved from a dark, amber-colored citrine. Here, the 18-karat gold dead tree trunk serves to support both the bear reaching for the honeycomb as well as the bee's nest attached to a limb. The simplicity of this group is heightened by the absence of leaves, which would detract from the drama and focus. The composition is arranged along two parallel spaces, one for the tree trunk and the other for the bear and honeycomb, cleanly delineating the tension in the group. Will the bear get to the honey or, given the precarious angle of the tree, will the weight of the bear topple the tree trunk? Resting inside the bee's nest is the Queen Bee, while three worker bees are perched on top of the Kalahari jasper beehive. The bees detach and can be worn as scatter pins. The bear, tree, and honeycomb are set on top of an orbital dial clock, mounted onto a rutilated quartz base. This remarkable group functions on many levels. For pure visual enjoyment, it is a beautiful sculpture in its own right; parts of it can be worn as jewelry; and, the wonderful group also tells time. It truly goes beyond anything that has been created, with its several functional parts combining as an exceptional sculpture.

The Wasp Tree (fig. 130) can also be appreciated on many levels. It functions as a sculpture with an outdoor setting of a tree with wasps. Like in the Bear Tree, there is a knurled dead tree (here in sterling silver) at the center of this sculpture, serving as a gathering place for wasps. The tree is "planted" into grass carved from British Columbian nephrite. The 18-karat gold wasp nest hangs from a branch and is realistically portrayed, featuring many layers with air pockets in between and an entrance at the bottom below rows of cells. The four 18-karat gold wasps on the tree have bodies of two-color brown translucent enamel and wings of plique-à-jour enameling. Each wasp body opens to reveal a small photograph compartment. Like the Bear Tree, in which the bees double as pins, these wasps also detach and can be worn as brooches. And, as if this were not enough, the entire tableau is set atop an orbital dial clock that commands a rather strong presence.

Von Zadora-Gerlof has also created a more formal clock, which he set in the middle of a citrine obelisk and flanked by citrine lions as part of a mantle garniture (fig. 131). Also known as *garniture de cheminée*, mantle garnitures are sets of ornaments for a chimney. In the seventeenth century they consisted of a few small porcelain pieces and, later, became more elaborate with the addition of silver items. In the late eighteenth century, the combination of a clock with two matching candlesticks became popular. Von Zadora-Gerlof has adapted this theme with the traditional clock in the center flanked by lions on either side. These lions are not depicted as his other sculptures, holding crests, but in a resting position with their front paws and tails overlapping the edge of the base. The artist has sculpted these figures to a fine level of realism, detailing muscles, bones, and even every strand of fur on the lions.

Although not a clock, the turtle sculpture (figs. 132, 133) features an 18-karat gold replica of a celestial armillary sphere and perpetual calendar on which any past and future dates can be read. An armillary sphere is an ancient instrument consisting of an arrangement of concentric rings that can be independently rotated on three mutually perpendicular axes to replicate relative orbital positions of celestial bodies relative to an observer on earth. A primitive instrument by today's standards, it was at one time an essential navigational aid as well as an effective tool for teaching astronomical concepts. In this piece, the instrument is mounted atop a turtle sculpted out of citrine from Brazil. The original drawing (fig. 132) depicts a cheerful version of the turtle with its head held up and one front leg raised. The actual sculpture portrays the turtle laboring to walk under the weight of the armillary sphere. Unable to raise its front legs, it pushes along with its hind legs. Von Zadora-Gerlof made a limited series of only six of the turtle-with-armillary sculptures.

Von Zadora-Gerlof's clocks are beautiful, elegant, and enchanting and almost seem transported from a fantasy land. Animals, amphibians, and aquatic life bring life to these pieces and a smile to the face of the viewer, who will also look at them to find out what time it is.

132

CHAPTER 5

NATURE-INSPIRED
JEWELRY

There have been a few time periods in history when jewelry was treated as more than just adornment, when it became more than simply a vehicle for the display of precious gemstones. For the most part, jewelry designers have followed a traditional course, relying on shapes inspired by ornamentation from fashion and the decorative arts. With the exception of ancient jewelry styles, which sometimes used animal forms, figural jewelry did not appear until the Renaissance, when animal shapes often included bodies made out of baroque pearls. Jewelry in novelty shapes would not be popular again until the second half of the nineteenth century, a time of exploration and discovery in the natural sciences and also a time when flora and fauna symbolized personal sentiments. During that time just about every form of insect, reptile, animal, and plant was used in jewelry design. Bees, beetles, dragonflies, grasshoppers, and butterflies crawled all over hats and veils, while lizards and serpents were fashioned into brooches or were worn around wrists, necks, or fingers. Novelty jewels featured hens, birds, mice, dogs, bears, and fish, while the chrysanthemum, iris, fuchsia, and orchid were naturalistically replicated using multi-colored enamels.

By the end of the century, art nouveau jewelers and artists continued to draw upon nature for inspiration but, instead of imitating it in a realistic manner, opted for impressionistic representations. René Lalique, the undisputed leader of this style, created spectacular jewelry incorporating molded glass and gemstones. His designs are often shocking in their approach to motifs, materials, and scale, seeming to go far beyond accepted boundaries.

Early in this century, during the Edwardian and art deco periods, figural motifs were superseded by swags and bowknots or by circles, squares, and rectangles. In the 1930s, Paul Flato and René Boivin reintroduced fanciful versions of nature, followed in the 1940s by Cartier and Van Cleef & Arpels, who offered dramatic representations of animals and

135

134. Rhododendron necklace, 1994. Pink and green tourmaline, canary and white diamonds, cabochon rubies, 18-karat gold; diameter: 7 1/2″. The flowers and bee on this necklace are fashioned so that they move when worn.
135. Frog Prince brooch, 1987. Green beryl, cabochon rubies, orange diamonds, white diamonds, 18-karat gold; diameter: 2 7/8″, height: 1 1/4″.

136. Frog ring, 1996. Green beryl, 20-karat gold, cabochon rubies, canary diamonds, 18-karat gold; length of frog: 1 1/2". The frog on this ring looks like he is about to leap off the wearer's finger.

137. Frog brooch, 1993. Green beryl, pink tourmaline, cabochon rubies, canary diamonds, 18-karat gold; length: 2 3/4". This brooch was specially designed for a client to give to his wife on Valentine's Day.

138. Frog stick pin, 1988. Green tourmaline, pink diamonds, 18-karat gold; length: 1/2".

birds. In the 1950s, Fulco di Verdura and Jean Schlumberger designed jewelry based on marine life and animals. In the following decade, Sterle created striking birds. In the meantime, David Webb came out with a line of jewelry featuring horses, bulls, elephants, and frogs that remains popular to this day.

136

Andreas von Zadora-Gerlof's repertoire of motifs from nature certainly fits into this long line of illustrious jewelry designers who have used jewelry to make pieces that are fun on the one hand and artistically conceived on the other. His creations have the added touch of a very personal imprint since he carves all the gem material that he incorporates into his designs. His talent is indeed rare in today's world, where manufacturing has taken over handwork.

Von Zadora-Gerlof brings to his jewelry designs the same artistic appreciation of the natural world that he does to the other areas of his oeuvre. Animals, birds, reptiles, amphibians, marine life, and flowers are sculpted out of gem material similarly to his sculptures, albeit on a smaller scale in keeping with the intended purpose of a piece of jewelry. Like his sculptures, his jewelry is conceived three-dimensionally and, because of his attention to realistic detail, it invites tactile as well as visual enjoyment. Wearing a piece of his jewelry attracts immediate attention.

137

The frog has remained a continuous source of inspiration to von Zadora-Gerlof both as a figure that he personally enjoys sculpting as well as one frequently requested by his clients. Its physical proportions are suitable for objects meant to be worn and, with a bit of artistic license, its appearance can be modified with lumps or warts to add another dimension to the surface. In all his frog-inspired jewelry, the creature itself dominates the design, usually with minimal supporting goldwork in evidence.

His frogs can be serious or whimsical, naturalistic or fanciful. Sometimes he borrows an image from his other works. For example, he took the theme of the Frog Prince sitting astride snails or perched on toadstools from his sculptural groups, clocks, and bronzes, and made it the central focus on pieces of jewelry. Instead of the Frog Prince ruling his land from a modified throne, the frog now sits on a lily pad or a ring shank, or holds a heart; nevertheless, he retains the essential symbol of his reign: a gem-set crown on his head.

On one brooch (fig. 135) the Frog Prince crouches on a gold lily pad, ready to spring up at the slightest sound. The lily pad is textured to simulate the actual leaf and, to add further interest, von Zadora-Gerlof has placed a

138

139. Tree frog brooches, 1994. Mexican fire agate, tsavorite, canary diamonds, 18-karat gold; length: 4″. The shapes of the Mexican fire agates are perfect for the backs of these frog scatter brooches.

pavé diamond ball to simulate a water drop. This brooch was specially created for the Forbes Magazine Galleries exhibition in 1992 and was bid at a silent auction to benefit both The New-York Historical Society and the Juvenile Diabetes Society.

On both a ring (fig. 136) and a brooch (fig. 137), canary diamonds are set into the backs of frogs for additional color and to accentuate the contours of their bodies—one smooth, the other lumpy. On the ring, the frog sits atop stylized gold leaves on the shank. On the brooch, the frog holds a pink tourmaline between its forelegs. Both pieces of jewelry are carved from beryl, a gem material that the artist favors for aquatic forms.

Von Zadora-Gerlof also created a pair of frog cuff links out of beryl with the amphibians in a crouching position (fig. 142). At a quick glance, the subject matter and pose are reminiscent of pieces designed by David Webb. However, the conception of each is very different. The Webb links are gold with green transparent enamel while von Zadora-Gerlof's amphibians are carved from beryl, a translucent gem material that allows light into the stone, with the result that the frogs seem to glow from within, making them more luxurious. They are available only in a limited number. Most of his jewelry is one-of-a-kind, although he has made—in editions of ten or twenty—multiples of a few. In this, his approach is similar to Jean Schlumberger, who also limited his jewelry production at Tiffany & Co. to a small number of pieces.

At one-half inch in length, the frog stick pin (fig. 138) is the smallest object the artist has created. It depicts a tree frog with gold feet splayed out in front and to the side, and

140

140. Tree Frog Prince brooch
and tree frog ear clips, 1988.
18-karat gold, cabochon rubies,
white diamonds; length of Frog
Prince: 2".

141. Tree frog brooch, 1997.
18-karat gold, translucent enamel,
diamonds, cabochon sapphires;
height 2".

141

is sculpted from a very fine piece of tourmaline that, like beryl, is translucent. Along with beryl and tourmaline, von Zadora-Gerlof uses another gemstone, tsavorite, for his frog jewelry. Tsavorite is a green-to-emerald-colored variety of garnet that was discovered in 1974. Instead of carving the entire brooch (fig. 143) out of one piece of stone, he embeds cabochons into an 18-karat-gold body to simulate not only the frog's color but also its warty skin. The enlarged ruby cabochon eyes seem to bulge out of the frog's head, just like on the living model. This brooch was commissioned by a client to present to his wife along with a complementary bangle bracelet in fish form, also set with tsavorite cabochons to simulate fish scales.

Von Zadora-Gerlof has used tsavorite on other frog jewelry where, instead of featuring it prominently, he artfully sets it so as to accentuate the colors of another stone. The eyes of the tree frog brooches (fig. 139) are tsavorite, their green coloration complementing the Mexican "fire agates" set onto their backs. "Fire agate" is a rare, iridescent variety of chalcedony that has an almost opal-like play of color. As gem material they are seldom used in jewelry design. On these brooches, von Zadora-Gerlof designed the frogs with their legs splayed, which spreads out their backs, thus providing an ample area for the misshapen "fire agates."

Von Zadora-Gerlof's experimentation with new designs has occasionally led him to create jewelry without incorporating his trademark carved-gem material. On a few examples, he sets small diamonds into the backs of creatures or enamels the surface for decorative effect. On the textured gold body of the Tree Frog Prince brooch (fig. 140), diamonds mounted into the back give the impression of the warty skin seen on his other gemstone frogs. The bodies of the tree frog ear clips (fig. 140) have also been textured. He has artfully designed the ear clips in a whimsical manner with one leg of the frogs extended so that, when worn, the amphibians look as if they are trying to climb up onto the wearer's ear.

In 1998 von Zadora-Gerlof began a business relationship with the prominent New York City concern A La Vieille Russie, which specializes in jewelry and other objets d'art. For this new venture von Zadora-Gerlof worked with the proprietor, Peter Schaffer, to design a selection of enameled jewelry based on animals, amphibians, arachnids, and marine life. One of the most appealing of this group is the tree frog brooch (fig. 141), enameled in translucent colors of green, yellow, and pink that seem to gradually change colors when worn.

Since so much of the underwater world (i.e., plant life, many fish and some amphibians) tends to have a green coloration, beryls, tourmalines, and peridots are natural stones to use on aquatic-life jewelry. The peridot beads on a necklace (fig. 147) have been cut into

142. Frog cuff links, 1998. Green beryl, cabochon rubies, white diamonds, 18-karat gold; length: 1/2". The green beryl on these cuff links was chosen for its shiny quality that simulates the actual slippery skin of the amphibian.
143. Fish bracelet and frog brooch, 1984. Cabochon tsavorites, tanzanite, white diamonds, ruby cabochons, 18-karat gold; diameter of bracelet: 2 3/4", length of brooch: 2".

143

142

144. Goldfish brooch, 1987. Star sapphire, white diamonds, 18-karat gold; length: 2 1/2".

145. Hippocampus brooch, 1992. Aquamarine, canary diamonds, 18-karat gold; height: 4".

145

146. Sea-life brooch collection, 1990. Seahorse: aquamarine, pearls, white diamonds, cabochon ruby, 18-karat gold; height: 2 3/8". Fish: rubelite tourmaline, pearls, white diamonds, 18-karat gold; length: 3". Crab: red tourmaline, white diamonds, 18-karat gold; width: 2 3/4".

147. Aquatic life necklace, 1987. Necklace: peridot beads, yellow diamonds, 18-karat gold. Fish clasp: tsavorite, ruby, sapphires, emerald, white diamonds, green tourmaline, 18-karat gold; length: 3 1/2". Clamshell clasp: 22-karat gold, white diamonds; height: 1 1/2".

nugget shapes and polished to give a pebble effect, while the grassy-green color is reminiscent of the water-washed glass that one finds at the beach. Three yellow diamonds have been randomly set into each bead to replicate sand. For the fantasy fish clasp, the artist sculpted the fins, tail, and wave motif that washes over the fish out of tourmaline, while faceted tsavorites serve as scales. He finished the wave with diamonds set into platinum to simulate foam. As a further option for his client, he created the diamond-studded 18-karat gold scallop shell as a convertible clasp.

144

Von Zadora-Gerlof's fish are usually portrayed in motion, either swimming or, as seen on the trout on a buckle (fig. 177), having just been hooked by a fisherman, wildly flapping in mid-air, fighting to get away. The fish's determination in its struggle to free itself from its captor is faithfully depicted by the artist in a three-dimensional manner with shadows under the gills and beneath the fin. For this piece, he chose a multicolored jasper, reticulating it for scale and fin details.

The goldfish that forms a brooch (fig. 144) has been captured with its mouth open, seeming to "breathe" in its watery environment. The tail, made up of striated gold work with a row of diamonds in between, has been flipped around to the front and resembles a flower more than a fish's tail. The bulging eye is a greyish blue star sapphire.

Along with the green variety of tourmaline, von Zadora-Gerlof also uses reddish tones of the gem for his underwater sea-life brooches. He designed two such pieces, along with

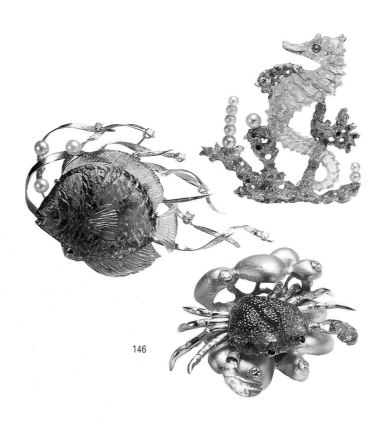

146

an aquamarine brooch, for a client (fig. 146). He sculpted the body and claws of the crab out of red tourmaline and chose the same material for the fish, carving its tail and fins from the outer, thinner part of the stone, which appears almost as transparent as glass. The third brooch in this series, the sea horse, is sculpted from aquamarine. Each of the sea forms on these three brooches is set within a modified underwater environment. The fish swims amid seaweed, with pearls and diamonds affixed to the blades; the crab is set into a shelf within a coral reef; and the sea horse wraps his tail around seaweed, anchoring itself to the sea bottom while water bubbles in the form of pearls rise to the surface. Within the confines of jewelry, the artist has been able to capture the essence of underwater life on these three brooches.

Von Zadora-Gerlof favors aquamarines with blue coloration, especially those stones with uniform color distribution throughout the gem material. Such is the case with the aquamarine he carved for the fish-like lower body of the hippocampus brooch (fig.145). The stone segment tapers as it curves from the top to the bottom, its surface finished with scales. The 18-karat gold head, forelegs, and tail are textured. For contrast, the hooves, the two top rows of scales above the aquamarine, and the scales at the bottom, between the tail flaps, as well as an elongated, spiral shell on the animal's forehead are polished gold. For added detailing, a vein has been added to the side of its face. At nearly five inches in height, this part-horse part-dolphin brooch is a stunning piece of jewelry. The artist has created two other brooches with the same likeness, replacing the aquamarine with green beryls. This image has also been incorporated into a sculptural clock group (see fig. 118) where the hippocampus is set into an underwater environment with seaweed and fish.

The reptilian contingent in von Zadora-Gerlof's repertoire of nature-inspired jewelry motifs is represented by crocodile, gecko, and lizard brooches (fig. 148), as well as a matching bracelet and ring set featuring a snake motif (fig. 155). The light green jadeite crocodile was originally created as a small tabletop sculpture. When the wife of the client decided to wear it, Von Zadora-Gerlof added a pin mechanism and a diamond-set collar to show that she had "collared" it. The reptile's body has been finished with scaly-skin detailing while the mouth has been lined with rhodochrosite with white jasper teeth.

The lizard has a long and illustrious history. In ancient Rome it was the symbol of wedded bliss. Resurrected as a motif at the end of the nineteenth century, when novelty jewelry was the rage, it was frequently enameled or gem-set; the most desirable

148. Reptile brooches, 1987. Crocodile: light green jadeite, rhodochrosite, white jasper, brown diamonds, 18-karat gold; length: 3 1/4". Lizard: green tourmaline, cabochon rubies, 18-karat gold; length: 2 3/4". Gecko: 18-karat gold, blue sapphire, cabochon yellow sapphires, length: 3 1/2".

149. Boar's-head cuff links, 1998. Labradorite, yellow and white diamonds, 18-karat gold; length: 1". The inspiration for these cuff links came from an antique scarf pin. Other versions include one in chalcedony and another with pavé diamonds.

149

150. Heraldic brooches, 1992. Lion: 20-karat gold, emeralds, rubies, sapphires, white and yellow diamonds; height: 2 1/2″. Griffin: 20-karat gold, emerald, rubies, white diamonds; height: 2 1/2″. Dragon: 20-karat gold, sapphires, rubies, emeralds, yellow diamonds; height: 2 1/2″. This group of brooches is part of a series of ten. 151. Lion bracelet, 1990. Black jade, yellow and white diamonds, cabochon orange sapphires, 18-karat gold; diameter: 3 1/2″.

designs are those with demantoid garnets along its back. Von Zadora-Gerlof has recreated this age-old image but, instead of making it in gold, he sculpted the body from a green tourmaline with its tail curled part way around. The stone is mounted onto an 18-karat gold support, finished as expertly on the reverse as on the obverse. The detailing on the lizard's body has been continued onto the gold tip of the tail.

The gecko, found mainly in the tropics, is a symbol for good luck. For the body of this reptile von Zadora-Gerlof designed a textured 18-karat gold body and set a faceted sapphire into its head. The sapphire, with its magnificent blue color, has been called the "gem of gems," an adornment fit for kings. It, like the diamond, was thought to reconcile discord; the artist's placement of it on the head of the gecko reinforces this symbolism.

A recent addition to von Zadora-Gerlof's menagerie is a bracelet watch in snake form (fig. 155). The snake was a common design motif in nineteenth-century jewelry due in large part to the choice of a coiled snake for Queen Victoria's wedding ring. Coiled bracelets and necklaces abounded, wrapped around wrists and necks. In von Zadora-Gerlof's piece the head of the snake opens to reveal a platinum and diamond watch. Cabochon rubies form the eyes, and white diamonds are set into the bezel and around the dial. The bracelet watch is made out of 18-karat gold with guilloche enamel articulated sections.

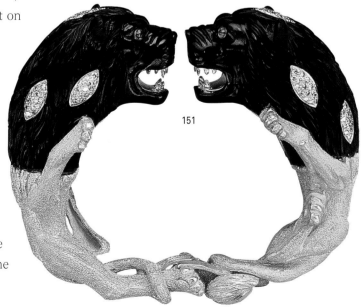

151

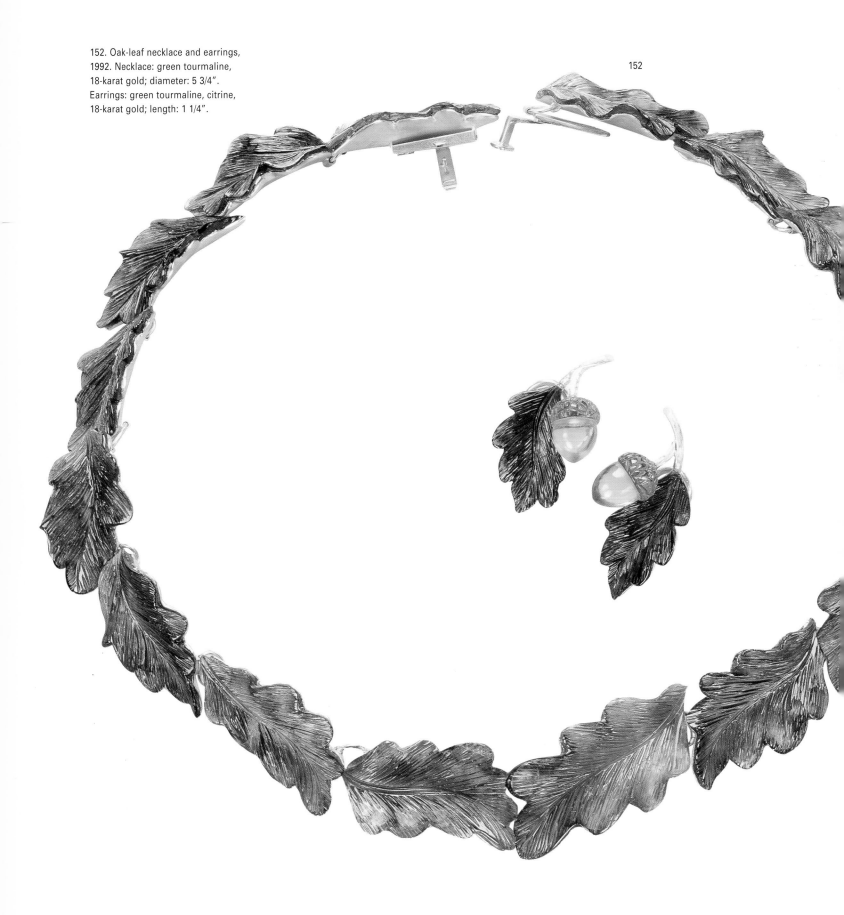

152. Oak-leaf necklace and earrings,
1992. Necklace: green tourmaline,
18-karat gold; diameter: 5 3/4".
Earrings: green tourmaline, citrine,
18-karat gold; length: 1 1/4".

153

153. Pansy necklace, 1990.
Amethyst, green tourmaline,
diamonds, 18-karat gold;
diameter: 6″.

154. Raspberry brooch, 1985. Green and pink tourmaline, citrines, 18-karat gold; length: 5".

155. Snake bracelet watch, 1998. 18-karat gold, white diamonds, cabochon rubies, 18-karat gold, guilloche with blue and green transparent enamel; diameter: 3". When the client ordered this bracelet watch and matching ring, she requested a snake design that surpassed anything that had ever been made.

155

154

The jungle has been a rich source of inspiration for von Zadora-Gerlof, one that he draws upon from time to time. In other areas of his oeuvre, he has created hardstone sculptural groups with monkeys, parrots, lions, hippopotamuses, and rhinoceroses.

The lion, as king of the jungle, is a subject jewelers have incorporated into their designs since ancient times. The first known examples of bracelets with lion-head terminals were made by the Assyrians in the late seventh century B.C. in a style that was later adopted by the Greeks and Etruscans. The fashion for these bracelets returned again many centuries later when mid-nineteenth-century archeological excavations unearthed jewelry in this style. In one instance, after General Luigi Palma di Cesnola discovered the Curium Treasury in Cyprus in 1868, he instructed Tiffany & Co. to make reproductions of several pieces, including a bracelet with lion's heads at the terminals.

In the 1960s David Webb created bangle bracelets with animal heads at the terminals. Enameled and set with diamonds and gemstones, they became immensely popular. Von Zadora-Gerlof continues this tradition of creating stylish bracelets that are both attractively designed and impressive to wear. When a client requested a strong design reflecting her love of Africa, he created a lion bracelet (fig. 151) in which the heads are sculpted from black jade and the mane inset with diamonds. The 18-karat gold textured bodies and legs are articulated to imply movement when worn. The lion's-head terminals face each other with their mouths open and about to leap at each other. The fierceness of the pair is reinforced by the razor-sharp teeth made out of jagged-cut white diamonds.

Von Zadora-Gerlof has also captured the lion in a series of heraldic jewelry (fig. 150). On the brooch the animal's mouth is open, roaring in true regal fashion with his shaggy mane cascading down his neck. He is atop a royal crown, set with ruby, emerald, sapphire, and diamond details. The other two images in this series are a griffin and a dragon, both set with precious gemstones for accents on collar and crown. These brooches, fashioned out of 20-karat gold, are hand-finished by Jim Hendrickson with minutely textured gold work combined with polished surfaces. They are truly works of the highest goldsmith's art. Only rarely does a jeweler take such care and patience to finish a piece of jewelry with this attention to detail, particularly in the late twentieth century.

Wild creatures abound in von Zadora-Gerlof's repertoire. He has a special knack for transforming a non-pretty animal into an object of artistic beauty. Such is the case with a pair of cuff links (fig. 149) in which the pose of the boars' heads is reminiscent of that of a trophy that a hunter proudly hangs on his wall. He chose to sculpt the heads in labradorite because its unique bluish-gray coloration resembles the coarse hide of the real animal. To further pursue the naturalistic theme he added a gold collar that at first glance seems to be a mere decorative effect, but in reality replicates the characteristic ring of light-colored hair around the neck of this species.

Nature teeming with life has inspired many great jewelry designers. Not only do they turn to the world of fauna but also to the world of flora. Perhaps the one contemporary designer who has been most influenced by the plant world is Angela Cummings, who takes a leaf or a flower and makes it into a beautiful, wearable piece of jewelry using traditional jewelry materials. Like this gifted designer, Andreas von Zadora-Gerlof looks at the floral and vegetal world and creates jewelry that is at once attractive

156

156. Grape-cluster cuff-link and stud set, 1997. 18- and 20-karat gold, green and purple transparent enamel; diameter of cuff links: 1". The theme of grape clusters was appropriate for the client, who loves fine wines.

157. Raspberry brooch in vase, 1985. Green and pink tourmaline, citrines, 18-karat gold, rock crystal vase; height: 7". The idea for a raspberry spray brooch that can also be set into a rock crystal vase was inspired by similar examples by Fabergé and Cartier.

157

Previous pages
158. Blossoms and birds necklace and bracelet, 1988. Necklace: citrine, green beryl, watermelon and pink tourmaline, pink, yellow, orange, and white diamonds, sapphires, 18-karat gold; diameter: 7 1/2". Bracelet: aquamarine, watermelon and pink tourmaline, white diamonds, 18-karat gold; diameter: 3".
159. Floral necklace and bracelet, 1988. Watermelon, blue, and green tourmalines, citrines, yellow sapphires, pink and canary diamonds, 18-karat gold; diameter of necklace: 7 1/4".
160. Rhododendron necklace, 1985. Pink and green tourmaline, pink, yellow, and white diamonds, cabochon rubies, 18-karat gold; diameter: 7 1/2". The idea for a necklace bedecked with rhododendron blossoms came about during a stroll through the client's garden.

to look at and lovely to wear. However, as in other areas of his art, he sculpts the main elements of his flora-inspired jewelry from gemstones. Most of his pieces in this series are important, one-of-a-kind necklaces.

Making exquisite gemstone flowers is a European tradition dating back to the Renaissance and Baroque periods. In the mid seventeenth century, the court lapidary, Dionysio Miseroni, created arrangements of gemstone flowers displayed in sculpted vases for the Habsburg Archduke Leopold Wilhelm of Austria. The Electors of Saxony also collected such gem-set floral groups. In Russia, this tradition was carried on in the eighteenth century with such pieces now part of the collections of the Hermitage and the Kremlin Armory Museum. Perhaps the one jeweler who is most noted for his gemstone floral arrangements is Peter Carl Fabergé, who was well familiar with these older works of the lapidary's art.

At the turn of the century, Fabergé made tabletop floral arrangements in which flowers were carved from various gemstones and the leaves from nephrite. These single sprays were most commonly placed in clear rock crystal vases, carved to appear as if they contained water. In the mid 1920s Cartier produced a selection of hardstone floral arrangements; however, instead of creating them in a realistic manner as Fabergé had

done, they utilized an impressionistic style. Cartier then placed the arrangements within rectangular glass vitrines to highlight their importance as works of art. All of these were intended for display, none as a piece of wearable jewelry.

Andreas von Zadora-Gerlof is the first decorative artist to create gemstone flower and plant motifs for wearable jewelry that meets the standards of design and execution set by his illustrious predecessors in the glyptic arts. No one has ever created gemstone floral jewelry in which sprays look like real corsages and necklaces look like real wreaths that wrap around a woman's neck as if the branches, leaves, and flowers were natural. His is the jeweler's art at its best.

Like Fabergé and Cartier, von Zadora-Gerlof created a spray but instead of flowers he filled it with raspberries (fig. 154) to be placed in a rock crystal vase that appears to hold water (fig. 157). Unlike those of his predecessors, this spray serves a dual purpose. It functions as a tabletop sculpture, but can also be removed from the vase and worn as a brooch. The artist has depicted this bunch of raspberries naturalistically, taking into account the reality that not every berry is ready to be picked at the same time. Thus, ripe raspberries are sculpted from pink tourmaline while unripe berries are carved from citrine, with green tourmaline for the leaves. At five inches in height, the brooch itself measures about the same as Fabergé's tabletop floral arrangements.

Necklaces present an intriguing challenge to the glyptic artist. On the one hand, nature offers an almost infinite choice of models of flowers and leaves to replicate with an equally large selection of gemstones. On the other hand, the amount of work required to bring those delicate specimens to life in the gemstone medium, together with flexibility

161

161. Duck-head cuff-link and stud set, 1998. Multicolored tourmaline, white diamonds, 18-karat gold; length of cuff links: 1".
162. Pheasant brooch, 1985. Green tourmaline, brown and white diamonds, 18-karat gold; length: 4 3/4".
163. Pheasant-head cuff-link and stud set, 1986. Green and red tourmaline, yellow diamonds, 18-karat gold; height of cuff links: 1".

164. Pheasant necklace and bracelet, 1988. Red jasper, kalahari jasper, yellow jasper, labradorite, coral, yellow and white diamonds, 18-karat gold; diameter of necklace: 6 3/4", diameter of bracelet: 2 1/4".

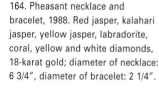

162

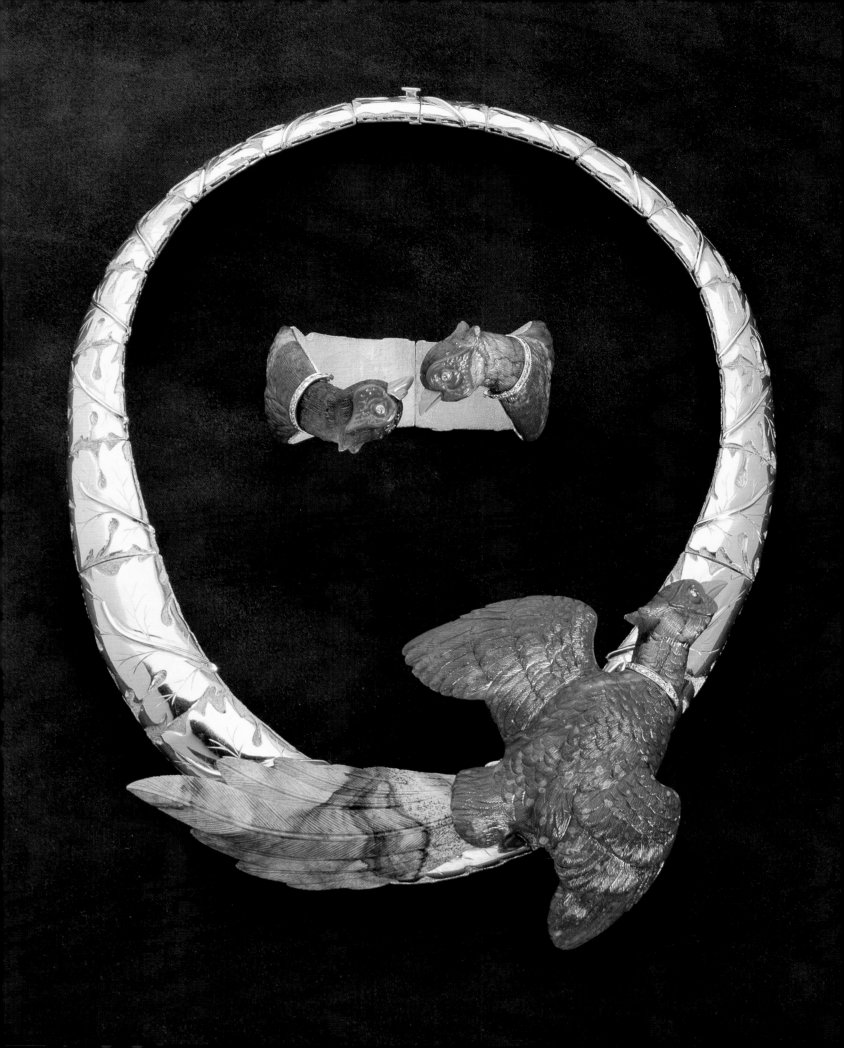

166

and other design demands associated with making jewels wearable, make this challenge almost insurmountable. The pieces described below are good examples of how successful von Zadora-Gerlof has been in meeting this challenge.

Because of its natural green coloration, tourmaline is an obvious choice for sculpting leaves, and fine specimens were used for the oak leaf necklace and matching earrings (fig. 152). He detailed each leaf with veining and made sure that the tourmaline used for a few leaves were lighter in tone around the edges, just like real leaves. The acorns on the earrings are sculpted from citrine. This necklace is reminiscent of the Greek gold oak wreaths, dating from the second half of the fifth century B.C., which were awarded to eminent personages, given as votive offerings on the Acropolis, or as prizes for the victors in music contests at the Panathenaea. On Greek wreaths, the leaves and acorns grow outward from a central wire, whereas on this necklace the leaves encircle the neck.

Von Zadora-Gerlof has designed a number of necklaces with life-size flower motifs. On the pansy necklace (fig. 153), flowers grow in decreasing size around it, with buds and leaves interspersed. The pansies are sculpted from a facet-grade, virtually flawless Brazilian amethyst. The stone was of such fine quality that the extremely thin blossoms could be carved without risking breakage. The design for this necklace was carefully conceived, taking anatomy into account for maximum comfort and also to show the flowers to best advantage. At the sides, where the necklace would meet the bridge of the collarbone, the artist placed two flower heads with petals curling part way under the blossom. The central flower, which sits at the top of the sternum, has been sculpted with flatter petals that curl slightly at the tips. Tourmaline leaves complete the design.

Von Zadora-Gerlof made two versions of a rhododendron necklace (fig. 134, 160). The flowers on both necklaces are carved from pink tourmaline from Maine with diamond-set pistils and stamens and with green tourmaline leaves. Both necklaces are designed with a clasp on which bees pollinate flowers and which opens by pressing on the bee's head. The flowers on the necklace are set *en tremblant*, so that they quiver when the necklace is subjected to movement; the leaves are articulated and the bee has moveable head, wings, and torso. With flower heads and buds growing in bunches around the necklace, and with leaves and buds falling in and out of the framework, it is a marvel in design and conception. With the exception of some of the jewelry designed by Rene Lalique at the turn of the century (using entirely different mediums), nothing has ever been made to equal it in design.

A plethora of multi-colored flowers adorn a necklace and matching bracelet (fig. 159). The floral motifs for this set were taken from those adorning the cloud on the sculptural group Angel World (figs. 34, 35). On the necklace and bracelet the various flowers have been carved in watermelon, blue, and green tourmaline, citrines, and yellow sapphires. Variety is also achieved through two different designs for the centers of the flowers, either with diamonds set on pistils and stamens or arranged in diamond-set clusters.

165. Parrot necklace and bracelet, 1988. Necklace: watermelon tourmaline, citrine, canary diamonds, cabochon rubies, 18-karat gold; diameter: 6 1/2". Bracelet: green tourmaline, citrine, canary diamonds, cabochon rubies, 18-karat gold; diameter: 3".
166. Hummingbird brooch, 1983. Watermelon tourmaline, pink diamond, 18-karat gold; length: 2 1/2". This brooch was ordered by a client who enjoyed watching hummingbirds in her garden. The artist captured the tiny bird in flight.
Following pages
167. Kingfisher necklace and bracelet, 1988. Necklace: green and red tourmaline, pink diamonds, 18-karat gold; diameter: 6". Bracelet: green tourmaline, yellow diamonds, 18-karat gold; diameter: 2 1/2".

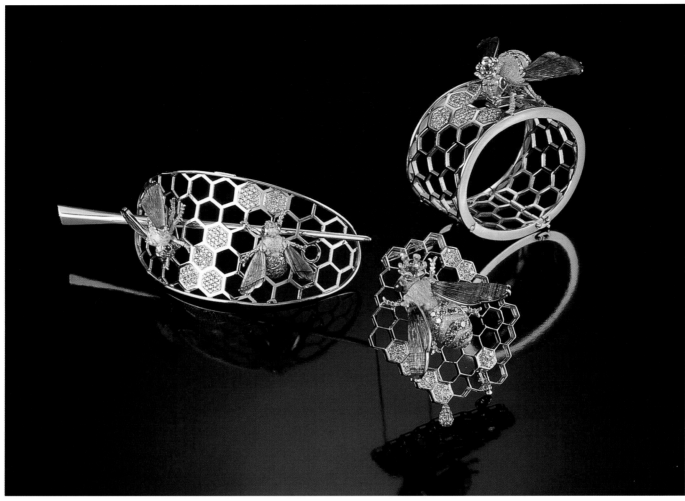

168

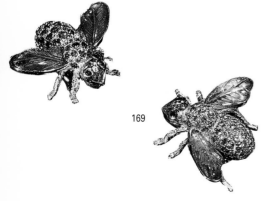

169

168. Honeycomb bracelet, brooch, and barrette, 1991. Bracelet, brooch, and barrette: 18-karat gold, yellow diamonds; Queen Bees: 18-karat gold, orange-yellow diamonds, watermelon tourmaline, cabochon rubies, multi-colored gemstones; length of brooch: 3″, length of barrette: 4″, diameter of bracelet: 3″.

Von Zadora-Gerlof designed a flower and bird necklace (fig. 158) for a client to give to his young, fair-haired daughter. The artist carefully selected gemstones that would complement the wearer. He did not want to overwhelm the young woman with dark, imposing stones or with an overpowering design. With these provisos, he created a necklace and matching bracelet with flowers and buds sculpted from watermelon and pink tourmaline, using 18-karat gold for the intertwining vine and leaves. On this necklace a citrine bird sits with its head cocked to one side while, directly opposite, another bird in green beryl roosts on a nest filled with four eggs, one each of either pink, yellow, or orange diamonds, and the other of sapphire. An aquamarine bird rests on a branch among the flowers on the bracelet.

The natural world has also served as inspiration for von Zadora-Gerlof's line of cuff link and stud sets. Cuff links are one of the few pieces of jewelry (along with a wedding ring and watch) that many men will wear. The rising popularity of French-cuff shirts has initiated a surge in demand as well as a desire for more interesting cuff links. Whereas many cuff links are designed along traditional lines and are quite conventional in their conception, von Zadora-Gerlof's links are never boring; rather, they attract attention. The grape-cluster cuff links and stud set (fig. 156) are enameled in the fruit's true colors, purple for the grapes and green for the leaves. In its conception and execution, this set resembles jewelry with similar motifs created by Louis Comfort Tiffany in the second decade of the twentieth century, either enameled or set with gemstones.

Von Zadora-Gerlof's cuff links can be worn during the day or, with the addition of matching studs, for any formal event. His jewelry for men is adaptable for any event. Since many of his clients are hunting enthusiasts, he created a selection of stud sets carved in the shape of heads of game. On one, he sculpted mallard duck heads out of multicolored tourmaline, the color of the real bird, with a collar of diamonds that closely replicates the marking around their necks (fig. 161). The ring-necked pheasant-head cuff links and studs (fig. 163) are made of green tourmaline with red tourmaline inset for the faces and a diamond-studded ring around its neck. The feathers are carefully delineated from one stone to the next so that the entire head appears to be carved from one stone.

The client who ordered the pheasant stud set is an avid hunter. For his wife, he commissioned a special necklace with a similar image (fig. 164). Von Zadora-Gerlof designed this special piece, along with a coordinating bracelet, with a pheasant whose body is sculpted of red jasper, with a kalahari jasper tail and labradorite head with red coral insert. This ring-necked pheasant, like the cuff links and studs, has a diamond-set circle around its neck. The pheasant can be removed and worn as a brooch, while the necklace of polished-gold sections with a leaf motif can be worn for less formal occasions.

The diamond-set pheasant in an almost five-inch brooch designed for another hunter is quite an impressive bird (fig. 162). The head was carved from green tourmaline, allowing for the darker area around the face. The gold body is set with brown diamonds for a stunning replication of the natural coloring of the bird. The pheasant is portrayed walking, with one leg in front and the back leg bent to take the next step.

The kingfisher necklace with coordinating bracelet (fig. 167) was ordered by a client to give to her daughter, and the inspiration came about in a truly serendipitous manner. While discussing this commission, the artist looked out the window and noticed a tree. He ran outside, broke off a branch, and returned to bend it around the neck of the client to show her how it would look. She was so captivated that she ordered it at once. The artist added two kingfishers perched on a textured gold branch that encircles the neck. A hinge at the back allows the necklace to bend as it is put on, and to be adjusted. The bodies and heads of each bird are green tourmaline, while the breasts are red tourmaline. The leaves, like his other flora-inspired jewelry, are carved from green tourmaline. Although this necklace is designed as a piece of jewelry, the three-dimensional birds are sculptural in their conception and surpass mere adornment.

The hummingbird has captivated artists as a design source for many years. In the 1860s and '70s Martin Johnson Heade traveled to Brazil, where he painted studies of orchids and hummingbirds in their natural environment. In the third quarter of the nineteenth century the hummingbird was replicated in diamonds and colored gemstones. There was even a fad, thankfully brief, for stuffed hummingbird heads and

170

169. Bee earrings, 1985. 18-karat gold with one earring of green diamonds and green tourmaline and the other of pink diamonds and pink tourmaline; height: 1".
170. Butterfly brooch, 1996. Watermelon tourmaline, canary diamond, 18-karat gold; height: 2". The colorations in this watermelon tourmaline perfectly capture the gossamer feeling of butterfly wings.
171. Queen Bee brooch, 1990. 18-karat gold, yellow and white diamonds, cabochon rubies, emeralds, sapphires, rubies; length: 1 1/2". The bee theme came about when von Zadora-Gerlof was working with a French client who requested a Napoleonic image of bees on a bracelet for his wife. The insect was so appealing to the artist that he began to make brooches with colored diamonds to simulate their furry bodies.

171

171

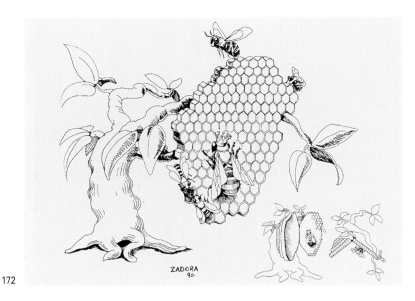

172

172. Preliminary sketch by Monica von Zadora-Gerlof for Bee Tree, 1991. Ink on paper.
173. Bee Tree, 1991. Tree: 18-karat gold, green tourmaline, yellow diamonds, rock crystal base; height: 8", width: 6". Four worker bees: 18-karat gold, canary diamonds, tricolored crystal, yellow sapphires. Queen bee: 18-karat gold, orange-yellow diamonds, yellow sapphires, rubies, emeralds, white diamonds; length: 1 1/2". When a client saw the sketch for the Bee Tree, he and his two brothers commissioned it at once as a special gift for their mother, who reigned as the queen in their family.

shoulders mounted on brooches and earrings, with a gold beak added.

More conventional designers have depicted the avian world in precious materials. The French jeweler, Sterle, created dramatic gem-set birds in flight with tail feathers and wings of woven gold. Von Zadora-Gerlof brings to this segment of nature his skills as a lapidary, carving a beautiful hummingbird in watermelon tourmaline (fig. 166). To complement the paler, pink part of the stone used for the head, he set a pink diamond for the eye. The artist also created a sculptural group (fig. 67) in which one hummingbird drinks nectar from an orchid while another sits on a branch. One orchid and one hummingbird may be detached from this group and worn as brooches.

Tropical birds are represented by a necklace and bracelet featuring parrots (fig. 165). Since both birds were sculpted from the same piece of watermelon tourmaline their colors are perfectly matched. They perch on an 18-karat gold vine necklace with leaves that twist around the wearer's neck. The parrot's head on the coordinating bracelet was carved from a very fine green tourmaline with a citrine beak. The artist also realized this theme in a sculptural group (fig. 68) depicting two parrots in an exotic tree.

The beauty of butterflies has captured our imagination almost since the beginning of time; to the ancients, the butterfly symbolized the soul. This delicate insect was a popular image in jewelry at the end of the nineteenth century, with interpretations of the wing markings portrayed in a variety of colored gemstones, opals, diamonds, and enameling. Art nouveau designers expanded on these designs, adding plique-à-jour enameling to the wings. Von Zadora-Gerlof brings to this special creature his sense of color and design and, of course, his superb lapidary skills. Instead of the common representation of the butterfly with its wings extended, as if pinned to a board, he designed the insect in profile as if flying, with its wings fluttering (Fig. 170).

Along with the butterfly, the beetle or scarab was another popular jewelry image in the late nineteenth century, due mostly to the opening of the Suez Canal and the discovery of ancient Egyptian tombs. Von Zadora-Gerlof readapted this theme but, instead of designing a traditional scarab, he depicted a large insect known as the deer-antler beetle (fig. 175). For the body he chose a unique blue tourmaline, while the legs, head, and menacing pincers provide dramatic contrasts of form and color.

The bee also appeared in late-nineteenth-century imagery, possibly because it was the emblem of the Bonapartes. Bees buzzed around veils or served as scatter pins, placed here and there. It was fashionable for Victorian ladies to wear multiple pieces of insect jewelry so one could have a variety of specimens from the insect world pinned to one's dress. The image reappeared in the middle of the twentieth century when figural motifs once again became popular in jewelry design. Fulco di Verdura created a

special bee brooch with a coral body and four enormous pear-shaped diamond wings.

Bees, like frogs, seem to be a favorite design theme for von Zadora-Gerlof, and are also often given royal status. He designs them to be worn individually or includes them as part of sculptural groups that, like his other ensembles, can be appreciated on many levels.

His bee earrings (fig. 169) closely replicate their actual shape, but the artist chose to use a different coloration for each bee. After all, stylish earrings do not always have to match (one need only remember the Duchess of Windsor's pearl earrings, in which one earring featured a black pearl and the other a white pearl). Christopher Walling took the idea of "reverse earrings" a step further when he created a pair of quince blossom earrings in which one grew upwards and other downwards. Von Zadora-Gerlof has reinterpreted this theme by designing color-coordinated bees in two colors. One bee has green tourmaline wings and a body set with green diamonds; the other has pink tourmaline wings and a body set with pink diamonds.

In the artist's frog world, he dubbed one as Frog Prince. He readapted this theme in the apiarian realm by presenting the Queen Bee with a crown, of course encrusted with precious gemstones. The Queen Bee's upper body (fig. 171) is textured gold to replicate that "furry" quality, while her back is set with canary diamonds and her wings are set with white diamonds.

174. Bee Hive, 1999, work in progress. Beehive: rutilated smoky quartz, Wyoming jadeite base; height: 6 1/2". Queen Bee: 18-karat gold, orange-yellow and white diamonds, rubies, emeralds, sapphires, cabochon rubies. For many years, the artist wanted to create a busy hive of bees. Some of them are depicted swarming around the hive while others are inside, making honey.

174

174

Honeybees are social insects that live in hives where workers build the nest, provide food, and care for the young while drones fertilize the queen, whose main function is to lay eggs. Von Zadora-Gerlof's glyptic works include several busy beehives in different formats, all of which have bees that can be detached and worn as brooches.

The Queen Bee appears as the decorative motif on a honeycombed photograph frame (fig. 111), and is featured on a jewelry suite designed with 18-karat gold honeycombs with hexagonal sections, several of which are filled with honey (really pavé canary diamonds) (fig. 168). On the bracelet, brooch, and barrette the wings of the Queen Bee are made out of watermelon tourmaline.

Perhaps the most spectacular of von Zadora-Gerlof's bee jewelry is the Bee Tree (fig. 173). It, like many of his sculptural groups, is a wonderment of imagination. The idea came to the artist while he was driving down the California coast with his wife, Monica. He had just completed a bee necklace and a very fanciful Napoleon-inspired bracelet. The royal symbolism of the bee, its association with creative activity and wealth, and its appearance intrigued him, inspiring him to conceive a hive sculptural group. Monica quickly sketched a honeycomb that could open up, revealing workers, drones, and a queen (fig. 172). When realized in gold and gemstones, this new ensemble elevated the artist's sculptural compositions to a new level.

A honeycomb with pavé yellow diamond honey hangs from the branch of the knarled 18-karat gold Bee Tree, with green tourmaline leaves atop a rock-crystal base. Three worker bees have tricolored crystal wings, while the drone and queen have yellow sapphire wings. The honeycomb opens, allowing the bees to climb in or out of the honeycomb or fly away to be worn as scatter pins. A queen will also be part of a Beehive currently being made (fig. 174). The conical hive of rutilated smoky quartz is set atop a table of Wyoming jade. The body of each bee will be set with canary diamonds and, in place of the watermelon tourmaline used for the wings of von Zadora-Gerlof's other bees, diamonds will line the wings of these bees. The queen will wear her multicolored gem-encrusted crown. Like in other sculptural groups, all these bees will also function as wearable brooches.

Like many great jewelry designers before him, Von Zadora-Gerlof turns to nature for inspiration. His muse almost invariably puts him in contact with the gentler side of nature, favoring plants and animals that please our senses and warm our hearts. The fidelity of his portrayals speaks not only of his superior skills and artistic sensibility and ethics, but also of his true love and respect for his models. Unlike any artist before him he sculpts the main elements of his designs out of gemstones carved by his own hand. He is, body and soul, a sculptor. In whatever branch of the glyptic arts he attempts, he leaves his imprint as a sculptor–in his case someone who creates beautiful life out of a chunk of gemstone. When looking at his oeuvre, assembled in just twenty years, it is almost unbelievable that one artist has created so much at the consistent level of excellence that characterizes all of his work.

175

175. Deer-antler beetle brooch, 1999. Blue tourmaline, brown and yellow diamonds, 18-karat gold; length: 3". The giant pincers on this insect intrigued the artist, who, after he decided to create a jeweled version, envisioned a large cabochon stone for its body.

• Alcouffe, Daniel, Margaret E. Frazer, William D. Wixom, and Danielle Gaborit-Chopin, *The Treasury of San Marco Venice*. Milan: Olivetti, 1984.

• Cavey, Christopher, *Gems & Jewels Fact and Fable*. Secaucus N.J.: Wellfleet Press, 1992.

• Fabergé, Tatiana, Lynette G. Proler, and Valentin V. Skurlov, *Imperial Easter Eggs*. London: Christie's, 1997.

• Fane, The Honorable Harry St. C., Hans Nadelhoffer, Eric Nussbaum, John W. Keefe, and Darrell Lee Brown, *Reflections of Elegance: Cartier Jewels from the Lindemann Collection*. New Orleans, New Orleans Museum of Art, 1988.

• Fisher, P.J., *The Science of Gems*. New York: Charles Scribner's Sons, 1966.

• Habsburg, Géza von, *Princely Treasures*. New York: The Vendome Press, 1997.

• *Fabergé*. Geneva: Habsburg, Feldman Editions, 1987.

• Habsburg-Lothringen, Géza, von and A. von Solodkoff, *Fabergé: Court Jeweller to the Tsars*. London: StudioVista/ Christie's, 1979.

• Honour, Hugh, *Goldsmiths & Silversmiths*. New York: G.P. Putnam's Sons, 1971.

• Hurlburt, Cornelius S., Jr., *Minerals and Man*. New York: Random House, 1970.

• Keller, Peter C., *Gemstones and Their Origins*. New York: Van Nostrand Reinhold, 1990.

• Lesley, Parker, *Fabergé: A Catalogue of the Lillian Thomas Pratt Collection of Russian Imperial Jewels*. Richmond: Virginia Museum, 1976.

• Long, Frank W., *The Creative Lapidary Materials Tools Technique Design*. New York: Van Nostrand Reinhold Company, 1976.

• *Lapidary Carving Design and Technique*. New York: Van Nostrand Reinhold Company, 1982.

• Massinelli, Anna Maria, and Filippo Tuena, *Treasures of the Medici*. New York: The Vendome Press, 1992.

• Menzhausen, Joachim, *The Green Vaults*. Leipzig: Edition Leipzig, 1970.

• Morassi, Antonio, *Art Treasures of the Medici*. London: The Abbey Library, 1969.

• Nadelhoffer, Hans, *Cartier Jewelers Extraordinary*. New York: Harry N. Abrams, 1984.

• Rossi, Filippo, *Italian Jeweled Arts*. New York: Harry N. Abrams, Inc., 1954.

• Schumann, Walter, *Gemstones of the World*. New York: Sterling Publishing Co., Inc., 1997.

• Sinkankas, John, *Emerald and Other Beryls*. Prescottaz: Geoscience Press, 1989.

• Snowman, A. Kenneth, *The Art of Carl Fabergé*. London: Faber and Faber Limited, 1962.

• Sofianides, Anna S., and George E. Harlow, *Gems & Crystals from the American Museum of Natural History*. New York: Simon and Schuster, 1990.

• Sutherland, Beth Benton, *The Romance of Seals and Engraved Gems*. New York: The Macmillan Company, 1965.

• Weinstein, Michael, *The World of Jewel Stones*. New York: Sheridan House, Inc., 1958.

• Zucker, Benjamin, *Gems and Jewels - A Connoisseur's Guide*. New York: Thames & Hudson, 1987.

NOTES

1. Quoted in Daniel Alcouffe, "Classical, Byzantine and Western Hardstone-Carving," in *The Treasury of San Marco Venice* (Milan, Italy: Olivetti, 1984), 73.

2. *Ibid.*, 73.

3. For illustration of two chalices of Emperor Romanos fashioned out of sardonyx bowl, dating from the 1st century A.D. with later silver-gilt, gold cloisonné enamel, and glass additions, and the other with sardonyx bowl dating from the 3rd to the 4th century, with silver-gilt, gold cloisonné enamel and pearls, see ibid., 131, 136.

4. W.S. Heckscher explores this idea in "Relics of Pagan Antiquity in Medieval Settings," *Journal of the Warburg and Courtauld Institute*, I, 1938, 204-20.

5. For illustration of the gold Cross of Lothair II, set with gemstones, gold filigree work, a Carolingian seal, and a Roman sard-onyx cameo of the Emperor Augustus, see Robert G. Calkins, *Monuments of Medieval Arts* (New York: E.P. Dutton, 1979), plate 8.

6. For illustration of chalice of Abbot Suger of Saint Denis with agate cup, dating to the 2nd century B.C., with silver-gilt mounting and set with gemstones, see *ibid.*, 124.

7. Quoted in Géza von Habsburg, *Princely Treasures* (New York: Vendome Press, 1997), 57.

8. For illustration of a two-handled covered vase in sard-onyx with silver-gilt mounts, see Anna Maria Massinelli and Filippo Tuena, *Treasures of the Medici* (New York: Vendome Press, 1992), 39.

9. "Ten of the vases were fashioned of rock crystal, ten of jasper, and the remainder of amethyst, chalcedony, and sardonyx or porphyry," According to Géza von Habsburg in *Princely Treasures*, 64.

10. Quoted in Antonio Morassi, *Art Treasures of the Medici* (London: The Abbey Library, 1969), 17.

11. For illustration, see Géza von Habsburg, *Princely Treasures*, 68.

12. *Ibid*, 22. For illustration of white onyx cameo on a chalcedony ground of Cosimo I with his wife, Eleanora of Toledo, and their children, see *Ibid.*, plate 25, or Anna Maria Massinelli and Filippo Tuena, *Treasures of the Medici*, 75.

13. *Ibid.*, 24.

14. For illustration, see *ibid.*, 78,79.

15. For illustration of two rock-crystal herons by the Saracchi workshop, see Géza von Habsburg, *Princely Treasures*, 105.

16. For illustration and additional information, see *ibid.*, 190, 188-189.

17. For illustration, see *ibid.*, 193.

18. For illustration of "The Altar of Apis," see *ibid.*, 199, and for illustration of "The Obeliscus of Augustalis," see Hugh Honour, *Goldsmiths and Silversmiths* (New York: G.P. Putnam's Sons, 1971), 149.

19. Géza von Habsburg, *Fabergé* (Geneva: Habsburg, Feldman Editions, 1986), 74.

20. Géza von Habsburg-Lothrigen and A. von Solodkoff, *Fabergé Court Jeweller to the Tsars* (London: Studio Vista/Christie's, 1979), 78.

21. For information and illustration of the *Revolving Miniature Egg*, see Tatiana Fabergé, Lynette G. Proler, and Valentin V. Skurlov, *The Fabergé Imperial Easter Eggs* (London: Christie's, 1997), 124-125.

22. *Objects of Desire: The Art in Sculpted Gems of Andreas von Zadora-Gerlof*, catalogue of an exhibition held at The Forbes Magazine Galleries, November 1992, 2.

23. In the lost-wax process, a rubber mold is made to conform to the clay model and is, in turn, encased in a plaster outer shell or couche. The rubber mold, held in place by its outer shell, makes the first negative impression of the figure which is brushed with molten wax, making sure all the minute recesses are filled. The two sides of the mold are then clamped together and molten wax is poured into the hollow interior of the wax-coated mold. Next, a mixture known as fireclay is poured into the mold to make the core and, after it hardens, the plaster and rubber molds are removed, leaving the wax casting. The sculptor touches up the details before sending it to the foundry to be cast into bronze.

Before casting can begin, gates and tubes are attached to the wax model to allow the molten bronze to be poured into the mold and air to escape. It is then encased into a thick outer shell, completely covering the figure before it is placed into the oven, where the wax is baked out (lost) and molten bronze is poured into the vacant area. After the sculpture is freed from its outer layer, it is cleaned and patinated.

24. *Ibid.*, 14.